CAN ANYBODY STOP THE PAIN?

*Practical and Pastoral Lessons
to Help You Overcome Pain
and Find Healing in Life*

LEWIS BROGDON

WESTBOW
PRESS°
A DIVISION OF THOMAS NELSON
& ZONDERVAN

WestBow Press books may be ordered through booksellers or by contacting:

WestBow Press
A Division of Thomas Nelson & Zondervan
1663 Liberty Drive
Bloomington, IN 47403
www.westbowpress.com
1 (866) 928-1240

ISBN: 978-1-5127-3941-1 (sc)
ISBN: 978-1-5127-3940-4 (e)

Print information available on the last page.

WestBow Press rev. date: 4/26/2016

CONTENTS

DEDICATION

I dedicate this book to my ancestors, known and unknown, who have imparted "folk" and godly wisdom to their families, churches and communities for generations. Thank you for the insight and encouragement you gave. Thank you for the abiding belief in God's goodness, love, strength and grace in the hard places of life, a faith that I have inherited from godly parents, family members and friends who were touched by you. Your legacy continues in this work.

FOREWORD

The Lord Jesus Christ has once again supernaturally given Pastor Lewis Brogdon insight into a desperate and hurting world that is looking for answers. One of my greatest fears is now subsiding as God is raising up men of God such as this who will step beyond the trenches of the "bless me bless me message" and redirect ministry to a broken and tortured people both saved and unsaved alike.

This book is so vital to the body of Christ because we have become such great pretenders. Ours scars hurts, pains, and failures are covered and polished with church jargon and religious antics to the extent that Sunday morning is almost like Halloween. Our real identity is concealed and as long as it is concealed, it will never be healed. Pastor Brogdon through life experiences of hurt and pain now releases healing into the deepest parts of the soul and spirit that brings total victory and restoration.

Let me encourage you by saying that as you read this book, discover your hurts and pains, receive the instructions that are inspired by the Holy Spirit, and allow the healing power of God brings you to total deliverance and freedom. Thank you Pastor Brogdon for obeying the Lord.

Bishop Frederick Myles Brown
Pastor of The Faith Center Church,
Bluefield, West Virginia
Presiding Bishop of Communion
of Covenant Ministries International

INTRODUCTION

WHY A BOOK ABOUT PEOPLE'S PAIN?

It must be real nice to be an actor or an actress. One moment you are just an ordinary person and the next moment you are a super-hero, model citizen, government spy, or an evil mastermind of a plan to destroy the world. It has to be interesting for people to step in and out of various roles and yet lead your normal life. The good thing about being an actor or actress is that the life you lead in a movie is not real. If you are a bad guy in a movie no one really gets hurts. No one is sick. No one dies. Actors and actresses are not super-heroes, evil masterminds, or social outcasts. They only pretend to be those persons. On television, there is no morning after the big nights or consequences to face for your actions. It is all entertainment and fantasy. That must be real nice.

In life, people do not lead separate lives. They have to deal with the hard realities of life. I am writing this book to people who daily wrestle with real life challenges. This book is for real people who are not afforded the opportunity to lead one real life and another life without consequences or the risk of getting hurt. It is one thing to go through divorce on television and another to have to live through the pain of a divorce in reality. On television, someone is always cheating on a spouse but in the real world, infidelity destroys people, careers, trust, friendships and families. Today's world is not a fairy tale land where everyone lives happily ever after. We live in a world where happily ever after is replaced by one eye-opening crisis after another. If you do not believe me, just watch the news or read a few news-magazines for a couple of weeks. Better yet just pay attention to the things your family and friends are going through. Happily ever after is a far cry from the pain that is becoming commonplace in society. And our communities and nation are reminded too often that people are hurting. We experience the trauma of violence and despair that they unleash upon us at inopportune times. Unlike, television shows and movies where no one really gets hurt, you and I live in a world where real people are getting hurt. The church cannot close its eyes and ignore people who are hurting. Pain is everywhere and it is our calling to be agents of healing amidst the brokenness that is on display in the world.

In my mind, I can hear the question, "why write a book about people's pain?" This book began with God who first opened my eyes to people's pain eighteen years ago when I was a young pastor trying to figure out ministry and life. God took me on an eighteen year journey, teaching me in increments and seasons about pain and how to find healing. I gained wisdom during these years while serving churches as a pastor and also my years as an educator of ministers. The knowledge of Scripture, conviction about biblical beliefs and pastoral compassion are clearly linked to doing this work for so many years with God's people. But some of the wisdom and insight found in this book are a product of my own struggles and lessons God taught me over the years. God's word has been made flesh in my life so I share enfleshed words of wisdom to you. In these pages, I sincerely believe you will find help with your pain and wisdom that can help you on the road to peace and total restoration.

There are also other reasons I want to explain here. I wrote this book to open our eyes to people in pain. We lead such busy lives that we fail to pay attention to people around us. Close friends can be in severe pain without anyone knowing it. This has to stop. I hope to cause us to pay attention to people around us. Another point related to this is the very real possibility that someone may buy this book because they are in pain themselves. In the pages of this book you will find encouragement, hope, strength and wisdom that can help you take baby steps toward healing. A second reason for the book is to provide some insight and perspective into the pain people are experiencing. While it is important to pay attention to people in pain, what is necessary is to understand what they may be going through, what they may feel and think. I try to do this. I lay out a journey into the cracks, crevices, alleys, holes, and closets of the mind and soul in pain. I attempt to give voice to it and encourage others to reach out to them. The third reason is pastoral. I write to cultivate and nurture compassion in the church for people in pain. If we are going to be agents of healing we have to get over the fact that hurting people do things we may disagree with and dislike. We have to get over being in shock every time someone makes a mistake or falls into sin. Today leaders from all arenas, whether political, religious, educational, or entertainment are making horrible mistakes that have to be dealt with in the court of public opinion. Public figures entrusted with the responsibility to protect the public's interest are falling for the old but powerful temptations of money, power, and sex. But they are not the only ones falling into sin. There is rampant abuse in too many homes and thousands of people in this country battling secret addictions. Yes, these things are happening too often. It is almost tragic to see the level of dysfunction on display today in our world.

But there is a greater problem that I want to discuss. Today people have lost their sense of compassion for hurting people. When people fall, too many jump on the bandwagon to humiliate or punish them in the most extreme manner. As a society, we have learned to be disgusted by people who fail. We out them and shame them and sadly exile them in a variety of ways. These people do have issues but who do they turn to for help? Everybody is pretty good at stepping on the fallen but rare is the voice of one willing to help. The Bible records two questions that speak to the need to reach out to all people, even people in dire straits: "Am I my brother's keeper?" (Genesis 4:9) and "Who is my neighbor?" (Luke 10:29). If a person has a relationship with God, they will help all people on the sole basis that God has done the same thing for them. I am not saying that you may have done the same thing as the person you're disgusted by but I am saying that God has been kind and merciful to you in spite of your sins and shortcomings. People are not helped because they deserve it. They are helped because God loves them. So, in spite of anyone's ill actions, Christian people should line up to help. We cannot throw people away. We cannot pick what kinds of sin we like or dislike. We have to hate sin but love sinners.

I wrote this book to help people recover from pain. The book is not written to condone sinful activity, but to help fallen, hurting people to recover. Hopefully after reading this book, you can assess what in your past has hurt you, make the necessary adjustments, and move on with your life. If you want help, it is here for you. This book will not replace professional counseling or therapy but can provide practical and pastoral advice that can get you on a path to healing. After reading this book you may decide to see a counselor or pastor to follow up on some of the issues discussed in this book.

I really want you to know that there is life, there is good living on the other side of the pain and years of frustration. If you have ever wondered how you put the pieces of your life back together, then open your heart, your mind and enjoy this journey. Your life will never be the same again.

PART I

PAIN IS REAL

These three words, "I am hurting" give voice to an experience known by many today. Though simple, these few words speak volumes about the problems people face. People are hurting. In the deepest parts of their soul is pain, confusion, frustration, and disappointments from years of experiences. The cumulative effect of painful experiences has left them deeply scarred. They insult, abuse, and sometimes act violently against people in their families and communities. Do you see how it works? Hurting people hurt people. It is a bad cycle that repeats itself too often in the lives of people. Someone is hurting. When they are unable to cope with their pain, they eventually hurt someone else. Let me tell you something, pain is real.

CHAPTER ONE

HURTING PEOPLE HURT PEOPLE

Have you heard someone say this recently? "I Can't Take It Anymore." This saying is becoming a common response to compounded stress from weeks, months and sometimes years of pain. I have heard quite a few members of churches I have pastored say this. They were on the edge. They were on the brink of losing it. Maybe you are wondering what a person means by saying they can't take it anymore. Allow me to explain. The "it" is acting out the inner pain that is within. The "it" is the "I can't take my life anymore attitude." The "it" can be a rush divorce, a fit of violence, a frenzied moment, a hasty decision about an important matter, a forbidden night or a few moments of dishonesty. The "it" is becoming commonplace in our society. There seems to be a growing amount of people who can't take "it" any longer. We live and work along a growing number of people who are on the edge of losing it. They are one situation from a breakdown or an outburst.

Some people try a range of things to counter such feelings. They try to suppress these feelings or ignore that they feel they are about to lose it. Some may have tried to get help but if something happens to trigger or hurt them they may erupt. I have seen this in family settings, work settings, even church. Yes I have seen people in church lose their cool and end up fighting in the house of God. I knew that the event in church that triggered the violent response was not the real issue. No it was the end result of a lot of pain and stress that they have not coped with in their lives. So instead of addressing what's really wrong they decided to give up on trying to overcome their pain and were resolved to let their pain, their "it" ruin their life. It has become the story of our era, "I am hurting, hear me roar." No wonder domestic violence is a major problem in homes across this country. No wonder the rate of divorce is still high. No wonder child abuse, alcoholism and other addictions are common today. No wonder violent crimes are on the rise. And this is just the tip of the iceberg. People are hurting. But the deeper issue is the inability to cope with pain. Coping mechanisms are weak or nonexistent for too many people today who live on the edge of a fit or breakdown of some kind. What is difficult about our society today is that so many hurting people are unable to cope with their pain.

The "it" is pain. This is what people cannot take anymore. People are mentally and emotionally incapacitated and unable to handle the stresses and strains of life. Our society is filled with people with various dysfunctions linked to unresolved pain. Society is literally being torn to shreds by hurting people. The pain discussed throughout the course of this book is pain that people are unable to resolve on their own. It is these persons who eventually end up in some manner or another hurting other people.

Hurting people hurt people. This statement accurately describes the repetitive cycle of pain that too many people are caught up in today. Someone hurt will inevitably hurt someone else and the other person hurt will do likewise. Thus, the cycle continues. People are hurt everyday as a direct result of an encounter of some kind with a hurting person. A person who cannot cope with their pain will hurt someone else.

History backs up this statement. For centuries imperfect people have oppressed and destroyed the lives of millions because of their evil ideas about life and other people. Many times, these ideas are a direct result of unresolved issues in their lives. For example, some men who were abandoned and not loved by their father grow up to take their pain out on others. When people cannot deal with their pain they can end up hurting someone else. But that is not the worst part about personal pain. The great disappointment is that the one hurting does not relieve his or her suffering after they've hurt others. The pain only worsens it. This can become a self-defeating cycle that can play itself out in individual lives and families for years, even generations. It's kind of like a virus that is very contagious. One hurting person can continue to infect the entire world with pain one individual and situation at a time. It works like this. A person is hurting, usually because someone hurt them in the past. If they are unable to cope with their pain they will end up hurting someone else.

This is simply stated but speaks volumes about the situation that we all know too well. A person who is emotionally incapacitated, mentally scarred or continually depressed to the extent of emotional withdrawal will eventually, in one form or another, spread their pain to others. Sadly, it is usually the ones they love, those close to them, whom they will end up hurting. This is the very heart of the message of this book. If the pain is not stopped we will keep hurting each other. Think of it as an odd or accidental form or revenge. It is not that we intentionally get back at those we love but more of getting back at whoever and whatever hurt us in the first place. I do not know how many people whom I deeply and sincerely love that I have hurt because of past times when I was not able to cope with my pain. It is a terrible way to live. I am sure many of you can relate to this.

People hurt other people for a reason. And the reason is their own pain. I am not making excuses for people but I believe that is exactly what is behind the pain they bring to others. People hurt others because of deeper underlying issues within themselves. Something is wrong on the inside. Something happened in the past. Something is unresolved in their life. For as long as civilization has been around hurting people have been hurting people.

As I allude to earlier, the pain is not alleviated when we hurt someone else; it only worsens our pain. Initially we think if we can get back at who or whatever hurt us we will feel better. Ironically, it never works. People only feel worse when they hurt people. No one is vindicated. You have not gotten a load off your mind or settled the score. You have only buried the real issue behind an ineffective way to overcome pain. The truth is most people do not feel better after they hurt someone. They actually feel worse. It compounds the pain they are already experiencing and creates more emptiness. People who hurt live with an empty feeling that is like a hole in their soul. It is a hole that cannot be filled with the pain of others.

Let me illustrate my point. Have you ever been in a heated argument? I mean one of those knock down and drag out arguments when the insults go back and forth and back and forth, sometimes for hours. I am sure a few of you know what I am talking about. I want to point out something that happens during these volatile moments. Have you noticed that the longer the argument goes and the more it intensifies the worse the insults got? I bet you have never paid attention to this fact. Remember that the worse insults got, the worse you felt and out of hurt usually expressed as anger, you railed back one insult after another. Many times it reaches a boiling point which led to yelling, screaming, crying, and sometimes got so heated someone almost resorts to violence. After the fight is over there is a cool down period. It is a period of emotional withdrawal in order to process what just happened. During this time you realized, you were hurting more now than when the argument began. Things were said that you did not mean to say or did not need to say out of anger. Now you are hurting more than when the argument began. Things were said that you do not know if they were intended or accidental. So what began as an attempt to express yourself, more accurately your hurting self, ended up making things worse. That is what I am talking about. Our inability to deal with our own pain sets us up to hurt others and most of the time it will be someone we love.

There is a cyclical nature to this. Hurting people hurt people. When they hurt people, they only worsen their pain. That is what I have seen in twenty three years of ministry and that is what God showed in painful moments in my own life when I hurt people I love because of my own pain. It was a sobering revelation. So I have been through this myself and come out on the other side with some insights that can help others in pain. If you are reading this and are hurting let me tell you something. I know that sometimes it seems like all your efforts to make things better only makes them worse. And you are wondering why it seems like your efforts are in vain. Maybe the reason is unresolved pain. Maybe you worsen things and unintentionally hurt people because you cannot cope with the pain of your past. If that is the case then facing your pain and turning to God for healing can be the first step in escaping this vicious cycle that leaves everybody hurt. I have good news. There is a way out of this cycle.

CHAPTER TWO

LIFE IN PAIN'S PRISON

Let us begin what may be the most important journey of your life. If you want to make a full recovery from the pain of your past you will need to make some big first steps in order for the process of healing to begin. Like walking, recovering from past pain requires the patience of taking life one-step at a time. So let's get started.

It is very important for you to understand that since you have experienced pain you are probably under some form of emotional duress and maybe oppression. People in pain not only shut down parts of themselves to cope with the pain they also shut themselves up to protect what is left of their sanity and heart. One analogy I like to use to describe this is the experience of being imprisoned. Pain will lock you up. In some form or another, a part of you will be locked up as a mean to somehow cope with the pain. This is an understandable response to pain but it is not always helpful. Imagine being in a prison cell with an inmate like past pain. In this cell it is hard to get away from it. You wake up with it. You eat three meals a day with it. You go to bed with it on top of you or below you. You talk to it and share your personal space with it. Imagine such a thing. That is how close you are to your pain.

The real difficulty of dealing with this first step is getting people to understand and admit that they are imprisoned emotionally and psychologically. Their pain will hinder their ability to trust and keep them fearful of future meaningful relationships. Pain can hinder their ability to express their emotions in a positive light and lock them in their past. Pain can deceive them into thinking that life is not good. Worse yet pain can force them to hurt the people they love, wreck their emotional well-being, confuse their mind making it difficult to think objectively and keep their hearts broken. This definitely sounds like being a prisoner. It is no wonder these people have a difficult time functioning.

The rate of people being imprisoned in this country continues to grow. I believe it is something more to this growing trend than many want to believe. While it is true that this country imprisons people at unprecedented rates in human history, there is more to this issue than a system that wants to criminalize and exploit people. There are some people who repeatedly turn to crime because they prefer life in prison. The prison represents a place of security and stability that some cannot enjoy in the outside world. I believe that some hurting people share this mentality also. They build themselves a prison by locking their emotions, hearts and pasts away deep inside of them. Many find comfort in emotional prison because the pain they have experience and currently experience is so acute that they cannot trust. They will not dare open up and ask for help because many times they cannot trust. They have probably been abused or hurt by someone they used to be close to or sincerely trusted. So opening up is out of the question for them. The outside world is too unstable and too dangerous for them to come out. Thus their emotional prison becomes their place or refuge.

If you have ever met a person who is distant and aloof to any sense of relationship it is probably because they have been hurt and the only source of comfort they could live with was to lock up any contact with almost anyone. You cannot touch these people with a fifty-foot pole. They are out there! They find safety in this manner of life because it prevents any future possibility of being hurt again. Imprisoned persons will not involve themselves in relationships where they run the risk of future pain. They will not interact with people who hurt them or knew them before they were hurt. They may not take a second chance on happiness and will minimize their responsibility for some of their decisions. Both are not very helpful responses.

Pain has a way of taking all the courage you have. That is why your emotional prison is so comfortable for you. You are finally safe. This prison has become your new home. You are able to just stay home and protect yourself from any possibility of future pain. Maybe you have protected yourself or maybe you have just become a big coward. I know this can seem to be a bit rude so let me explain what I mean.

Life in the Shadows

People in pain imprison themselves. This is a way to describe an internal response to pain. But there is more.

People in pain also live in the shadows. I have found this idea of living in the shadows another helpful way to talk about people in pain because it draws attention to how they interact with the world around them. The shadows provide cover for their pain. This is why it is hard to recognize hurting people. They hide their pain in prison and live in shadows. They paint smiles on their faces and carry on like life is great. But on the inside they are in considerable pain. Smiling faces emerge from the darkness during the day so people can have some semblance of normalcy. They work. They go shopping. They go to church. They hang out with family and friends. They look fine laughing, working, caring for others, even worshipping God but there are things in the shadows that they wrestle with when they drive in the car, when they are alone, and at night when sleep eludes them.

People have grown accustomed to this way of functioning. People get up in the morning and paint smiles on their faces and go about their day. Now to some degree the strength to not allow stress and pain to consume your life is good. It is a part of learning life balance. But there is a danger in this when it becomes too routine. Masking our pain in the shadows does not set us on the path to healing. It only compounds our pain. Nothing is more difficult than not only dealing with your pain but also dealing with the fact that you have to go to great lengths to conceal it from others. Life in the shadows is a burden that no one should live under. While emotional prisons and shadows allow you to compartmentalize and hide your pain, there is an alternative. You can open the doors to your cell and turn the lights on and allow God's Spirit and capable counselors to help you experience healing.

Come Out Wherever You Are

Stop hiding your pain. You cannot hide who you really are and what you have gone through from everyone. You have to come out and face it. Well I have good news for you. You do not have to live this way for the rest of your life. You can get out of jail. There is life after tragedy and pain. You have so much to live for that you cannot experience behind emotional bars. Here is where the rubber meets the road. You have been hurt. It is not your neighbor, someone on television or someone you are reading about in the paper. It is you. Now let us deal with it together.

When you have been hurt you have a decision to make right from the start. Are you going to face the pain head on and recover over time or are you going to let the pain ruin your life? How do you face your pain? A good place to begin is admitting your pain to yourself and confessing it to God in prayer. It may provide some strength just to open your mouth and express your feelings to God. You may also want to find a trusted counselor like a pastor to talk to as well. If the pain is complex and deep you should talk with a therapist. Whatever you decide, I hope that you will face what has come into your life to hurt you knowing that it can eventually become a stepping-stone to better things. Pain can make you bitter or it can make you better. It is your choice as to how you will handle it.

Another important point is the understanding that you are not alone. Pain is not partial to any person. Everyone gets their fair share of pain and I mean everyone. When you are in pain, the temptation will be to exceptionalize your situation. There may be days when you feel alone. There may be days when you feel no one understands your pain.

While that may be true, it should help you to take some first steps to healing by realizing you are not alone. Many others share the pain of life with you in their own distinct way. Why? Because that is pretty much how life goes with billions of sinful and imperfect people living together and interacting with one another. The truth is somebody is going to be hurt. People cause pain. People hurt people. It is inevitable. I do not care where you go or what you want to do with your life, as long as people have anything to do with it, you will run the risk of getting hurt. You will get hurt because people are not perfect. Failed relationships, family problems, job stress and even the saints at the local church are just a few of the ways you can get hurt because people are involved. Accepting that hurt is one of the risks of life can help you feel connected instead of isolated.

Let us push a little further. If you are going to recover from the pain, you must not try to deny your pain. There is no need to pretend everything is fine. The reality is that it hurts to be hurt. There is no need to minimize your pain or to be ashamed that you are in pain. It hurts to be hurt. It is a very difficult and sometimes traumatic to experience brokenness of some kind. Pain is not easy to deal with and it can consume your mind for a season. It is tough stuff. It makes you cry. It makes you numb. It makes you crazy. It clouds your thinking. It also makes you react to certain situations in an irrational manner. So accept it. Tell God I am hurt. Tell people who love you I am hurt. If it takes looking into the mirror to accept this, do so, but by all means do not deny that your situation is real. I say this because a temptation I want you to be aware of denial. Some people who have been emotionally devastated go into denial. They can be utterly devastated by a life situation and carry on like nothing has ever happened. How do they do this? They do so because they are in denial. They somehow believe that everything is fine. It is a defense mechanism one uses to protect oneself. It may seem to be a good thing but eventually you are going to have to face reality. It is you. Now you have to do ask yourself, "What am I going to do?"

Going into denial, or pretending like nothing has happened or even sweeping it under the proverbial rug will not help you come to grips with the pain. The best thing to do is to face the pain with all the strength and courage that is within you. Deal with reality in a real way. If dealt with appropriately, you can recover. If you allow pain to lie dormant, it will fester and result in even greater pain. The Bible tells us that when we let the sun settle on our anger it gives the devil all sorts of territory in our lives (Ephesians 4:27). The same holds true when we allow painful issues to live inside us. It gives place to other evils. But if we face them and are truthful with ourselves, we have made the right step toward recovery.

Let My People Go

The next step may be the most difficult one to take. If you are going to make a full recovery, you have to forgive whoever hurt you. Now there is a great misunderstanding about forgiveness so I am going to explain what forgiveness is, what it does, and who it benefits. Forgiveness come from a Greek word (aphesis) which is often translated as remission or pardon. Forgiveness means to pardon someone. It means to release someone from a debt owed or a wrong done whether it was intentionally or unintentionally. Forgiveness is multi-directional in that it releases both the person who wronged you and the person wronged. While it is important to emphasize that forgiveness releases the one wronged so they are not bound to an offense, the implications go beyond the one who committed a wrong. Forgiveness does its best work on the one wronged and hurt. It liberates them from the prison pain will attempt to keep them in. This is why it is possible to restore relationships. When genuine forgiveness takes place, because the person wronged has been released, too, they do not seek revenge, wish harm or foster anger towards the person who hurt them. The offender is pardoned. They are released from their hurtful actions and it is possible to restore the broken or hurt relationship. The truth is forgiveness takes time and depending on the offense restoration is always possible. Forgiveness can lead to the restoration of broken lives and relationships but it is not necessary. A relationship does not have to continue for forgiveness to take place because the important thing is what forgiveness does in the spirit and soul of the one wronged. In the end, things should really get better after genuine forgiveness has taken place.

Now that all sounds well and good at the conceptual level but it is extremely difficult to practice. Forgiveness is not of human origin and it cannot be done by one's power. In fact, forgiveness is unnatural. It goes against one's natural instincts. The natural thing to do to one who harms you is to return the favor. People tend to seek revenge for wrongs done to them. Forgiveness is not natural, it is spiritual. It is a divine concept and a quality that God enables his people to exercise by the power of his Spirit. Forgiveness is not based on a person's merit because no one deserves to be forgiven. Instead, it is based upon the teachings of the Jesus Christ about the way God relates to us (see Matthew 6:12-15, 18:21-35; Mark 11:25-26). Jesus taught that everyone should receive forgiveness and his disciples should forgive people for every offense. One of the reasons Jesus came to earth was to model love and forgiveness for the world. Jesus provided an example of what forgiveness looks like and why it is important to forgive. John 3:16-18 provides a simple narration of this. God loved the world but the world had a problem. The world was in darkness and rejected God. But God was willing to pardon humans and give them another chance. So He sent his Son to provide forgiveness of sins so the relationship between God and humans could be restored. Once you understand the principle of forgiveness taught in the gospels and commit to living it by faith, one is able to forgive others. Committing to doing this by faith opens us to God's Spirit who gives us spiritual power to live this out. This is how a Christian can do unnatural things like pray for their enemies, love people who hate them and forgive people who hurt them. God helps them to do this. Otherwise, it is impossible.

Understanding that you are supposed to forgive someone does not help to actually forgive a person who just hurt you. Our real problem is that we are not willing to forgive a person who hurt us. Many want to talk forgiveness with their mouth but practice unforgiveness in their heart. They claim to have forgiven but spend hours and years of energy and precious time hating people. When you have forgiven someone, you honestly decide to let them go! That is what God is telling you, "let my people go." Stop trying to live with unforgiveness in your heart by your refusal to pardon someone who wronged you. When God forgives anyone who comes to Christ, he does not hold their sins against them. They are absolutely and totally released from the debt of sin and death. That is how God forgives our sins, which is totally different from how people practice forgiveness. Some people say they forgive you but hold such resentment and animosity toward you. Sometimes these feelings persist for the rest of their lives. That is not genuine forgiveness. God does not treat his people that way. So why do you do it?

People generally have a difficult time forgiving others because they think forgiveness is letting the one who hurt you get away with it. In your mind, you think the other person is getting away with everything. So you want them to pay for what they have done to you and therefore respond to them with anger and hate and animosity. But this is a big misunderstanding about forgiveness. God has established it so that when we sin, eventually we get what is coming to us.

> Be not deceived; God is not mocked: for whatsoever a man soweth that shall he also reap. (Galatians 6:7)

No one gets away with wrong. You will reap what you sow. Please do not view forgiveness as God's escaped from sin card, because it is not. However, God had decided to forgive people of all wrongs if they come to him and repent. You must also realize that it is not your place to be the judge, jury and executioner. That is God's place. When you choose not to forgive someone that is what you are telling God. Basically you tell God that you want to be the judge because he will only let them get away with their actions. And when you are hurt, I mean really hurt, you want to make the person who hurt you pay! Please understand that it is not up to you to decide who should be forgiven. That is God's choice and his choice to offer forgiveness to everyone. Now in his wisdom and knowledge of things that are not aware of, he will deal justly with people who hurt you. But again, that is God's job, not yours.

The real power and beauty of forgiveness is that it not only releases the one who is responsible for the painful situation, it also releases the victim from feelings of anger, resentment, and bitterness that can potentially become a hole they keep themselves in. While it is pain that hurts you, it is unforgiveness that actually keeps you imprisoned. The choice not to forgive keeps you in the prison of pain but forgiveness frees you from it. It is not so much the pain that sentences a person to a life of misery as much as it is their choice to share a cell with the very pain that hurt them in the first place. People who are hurt condemn themselves to a life of pain because they hold on to the pain and refuse to release it through forgiveness.

When you commit to forgiveness, you separate yourself and you free yourself from holding on to the pain. Once you do this, you are now open for God to come in and manifest healing in your life. You can forgive and let go of the pain that imprisoned you in the past or even the pain that still may have you imprisoned. But if you chose not to forgive, you basically carry the person around whom you despise in your heart for the rest of your life. Now, how much sense does that make? You choose to bear the pain and the person all at the same time. Guess what? You have not punished anyone, but yourself. You carry that pain around like you are doing yourself some good, but you are actually killing yourself. Let me tell you something, carrying forgiveness in your heart is much worse that anybody can do to you. Don't become your own worst enemy. Let them go.

I know that this is the big step. And I know that this is difficult. But it is the step you have to take. You have to forgive them. Let that person go. Whoever it is, they are surely not worth your demise. You will destroy yourself if you keep trying to hold people whom God wants you to release. Life cannot work with that stuff in your heart. Life will not work with that stuff inside you. The one who has the power to get rid of that stuff is you. God has given you the power to free yourself and set yourself on the path to healing. There is something liberating about forgiveness. It frees you to live. It says that I am better than the temptation to live miserably. It allows you to sleep at night with peace of mind. When you forgive everyone comes out with a much-needed second chance and valuable lessons learned to be shared with others. So when you let them go, you really free yourself. Let me bring this part of the discussion to a conclusion. First, remember, when you have been hurt you have to accept that it is you. Second, by all means, do not go into denial because the pain and the situation that you are in are not going away. Third, do not cover up your pain. It will only manifest itself at another time or occasion. Fourth, and more importantly, if you want to get out of the prison of pain forgive whoever hurt you. Let them go and by letting them go you free yourself.

CHAPTER THREE

WHEN YOU HAVE HURT SOMEONE

Every good movie has to have a villain. Some villains are so bad that you feel a little hate for them as the movie progresses. In fact, by the end of the movie you cannot wait until he or she gets what's coming to them. You feel a little joy when their evil plans fail. Imagine for a moment the role of the villain in real life. The truth is, nobody wants to be a villain. Unfortunately, there are those in society whose mistakes involve other people and they become real life villains. They are family members, friends, co-workers and sometimes leaders we looked up to at one point. Their actions have given them a role that no one wants to have because nobody likes bad guys or bad girls. It is hard to imagine just how horrible it is to be this person.

Nobody wants to be the bad guy because people dislike them. And social dislike often expresses itself as hate and disdain. Our society hates the fallen. We hate them because we do not like what they do. Nobody wants to be the cheating spouse. Nobody wants to be the one who went to jail. Nobody wants to be the woman who had her children taken away. Nobody wants to be the one who is addicted to drugs. Nobody wants to be the one who just lost his or her job because of misconduct. Nobody wants to be the dad who is talking with a police officer and social worker because he beat up his kids in a fit of rage. Nobody wants to be the one who loses the public's trust because of misappropriation of company funds. I am talking about real life. These are the people we love to hate and hating them is pretty easy. The difficult task that I want to challenge us to consider is having some compassion for these people. It is a difficult thing is to minister to these people's spiritual and emotional needs but that is our calling because God loves the worst of sinners and saints who do sinful things. We cannot just turn our backs on them because we despise what they did. As members of the church, we have a higher calling.

> Brethren, if a man be overtaken in a fault,
> ye which are spiritual, restore such a one in
> the spirit of meekness; considering thyself,
> lest thou also be tempted (Galatians 6:1).

Paul encouraged the Galatians to do this. The entire letter to the Galatians was written to people who were lapsing in their faith. So the apostle lays out a way to help people who stumble in faith and life. He says, restore people in a spirit of meekness. This is what I want to encourage you to do. People who fall and sin need help and ministry too. They need someone to reach out to them and show them compassion. I believe that is what God calls us to do. But that is a major problem we have in society in general and many churches in particular. We are becoming very cynical and cold. There is a general tenor of meanness that pervades social relations today. You see it on social media. You see it in traffic. You see it among politicians. Social cynicism often expresses itself in hostility. People lash out, act rude and even instigate violence. But often the primary manifestation of cynicism is indifference. How many times have you heard someone say "I don't care?" This sentiment reflects a mindset and practices that communicate indifference toward others. There are people who just do not care about others' well-being. This cynicism and indifference has affected the church, too. There is a genuine lack of compassion for perpetrators of pain. Church people are quick to discard and judge people who hurt others. They are treated like their lives have no worth from that point on. The church does this because it is following the lead of the world. Society does this all the time.

Nobody Wants to Help People who Fall

Many times when I watch the news and see those who have made terrible mistakes that became a matter of public opinion, I am startled by the lack of leaders who advocate for compassion, justice and care for victims, families, and communities impacted by sin of some kind on one hand yet compassion, forgiveness and restoration on the other for people who commit such acts. Many in the church do not want to help the fallen because they follow the world's lead instead of the principles of the gospel.

People blow it and make bad decisions that affect the lives of those around them. This is what is going on in the world. I am sure you do not like it. I do not like it either but we have to be able to deal with these problems and help hurting people, even if they are the bad guys. I want to be clear about this. I am not claiming that we should ignore the wrongs that people do and do not hold them accountable. I am not saying that at all. I agree that people should be held accountable for wrongs committed. Accountability should factor the people affected by what you have done and the effect of the wrong done. It is important and healthy to do this. What I am trying to underscore is the tendency to naturalize revenge and indifference. These are contrary to the gospel of Jesus. I will explore this in part here and in depth in a later chapter.

In a real sense, both society and the church need to grow up. The witness of the Bible is clear on human behavior. It gives abundant examples of the truth that human beings and human institutions are deeply sinful and there is no depth humans will not stoop to. Humans are capable of carrying out mildly problematic actions that only hurt themselves to horrible actions that affect others. This witness should inform our understanding of human behavior and strengthen our capacity to show compassion for people that do sinful thigs. I just do not understand all the shock when people do horrible things. "I cannot believe he or she did that" is a common response. Now I understand some of the shock because people experience grief when trauma is communal but some of the shock is exaggerated and unwarranted as if humans are not capable of duplicity and error. Look people, there was a reason Jesus had to die on the cross. He died because humanity is inescapably corrupt and sinful. Theologians refer to this as the doctrine of total depravity, which states that human are thoroughly sinful. But human weakness and sin does not have the final word. Jesus came to this earth two thousand years ago to help all the hurting, even the ones guilty of horrible sins. One woman caught in adultery was forgiven by Jesus. He did not stone her but gave her a second chance to improve her life. A thief was forgiven by Jesus and went to heaven. Jesus prayed that God would forgive the very people crucifying him. Jesus forgave Peter for denying him. Jesus loves and forgives the worst of all people.

So to the bad guy around the corner, there is hope because Jesus wants to help you with your pain also and he is calling his church to be that agent of healing in your life. I want to do two things in the rest of this chapter. I want to impart some wisdom to the person who may have hurt someone and I want to encourage people to have compassion for people society loves to hate. There are two things people need to know about familial and local villains. First of all, it is their pain that pushes them to do some of the things they do. Yes, they are selfish, irresponsible, reckless and maybe exploitative but many times their desperate and horrible acts of sin are cries for help. Please understand I am not condoning their actions but sometimes this is the case. There is something wrong inside them that leads them to do some of the things they do. From our study thus far, their problem is pain. They cannot cope and eventually inflict pain on others. Even though they hurt others, you must understand that they are hurting themselves. Secondly, you need to understand that when they do something bad, it hurts them even more. I do not know what it is in a person that causes them pain when they hurt someone. This is the untold story behind many local villains. Everybody hates them for what they have done and they hate themselves for their actions. In fact, their hurtful actions unleash deep feelings of self-hatred. I know there are some rare cases in which some people don't care who they hurt. But most of the time it hurts you to hurt someone in one way or another. This is another form of the same cycle of "hurting people hurt people." So look at it this way. They are hurting. They hurt someone else. They hurt even more for their actions. Playing this role is miserable in real life because everybody hates you for your actions and you hate yourself for your actions. It is like their actions carry their own punishment. They get punished more every time they hurt someone else. You see, this is why I wrote this book. I want to help even the person who is responsible for inflicting pain on others, even those they love.

If you are this person and need some good advice, here's what you need to do. First of all, you have to face the music. You blew it. You messed up. You hurt people. There is no other way around it. You have to come to grips with your actions. You must also take responsibility for them. Do not cast blame on someone else. You did it. And on that sour but healthy note, you make the choice to live your life differently going forward. That choice needs to become a life commitment. Otherwise, you probably will not change. Second, before you get all happy, you have to understand that there are always consequences for your actions. God forgives sin but does not erase consequences. Whatever repercussions are coming cannot be avoided. Life promises that our actions will bring certain consequences. And misconduct will certainly bring consequences that will be difficult to deal with at times. When you lie to people who trusted you they are not going to trust you again. Committing crimes will land you in jail. Abusing your children can result in you losing parental rights or custody. When you do hurt others, these are consequences, many which will live with you for the rest of your life. They will serve as a constant reminder of bad decisions. Consequences are results of your actions and they are unavoidable. Facing this is very difficult and painful. It is hard to see the fruit of bad actions and pain caused to others but very much a part of charting a new path in life.

Thirdly, you have to forgive yourself. This will possibly be the most difficult thing for you. It is easier to forgive someone else than it is to forgive yourself. When you refuse to forgive yourself you continue to hold anger in for your actions and the desire to punish yourself for your misconduct. Unforgiveness is a dangerous thing. If you do not forgive yourself, you will never be able to move forward with your life. Moving forward is an indication that you have some level of peace about the past and are resolved to do better in the future. But if you do not forgive yourself you will entrap yourself in a prison that you build and you will keep yourself locked up forever. Listen, yes, you blew it! You made a terrible mistake. Yes, you also have to live with the consequences for your actions. But, you have to forgive yourself and slowly move on. Because, unless God takes your life, it is not over yet.

A person who will not forgive themselves will constantly think, "How could you do this?" "I hate myself." "I'm so stupid." "I ruined my life." "There is no hope for me." "I am the worst person on the planet." With these thoughts running through your head, there is no room to be thinking about making improvements in the future starting now. Unforgiveness will trap you in the past. You have to get over it and forgive yourself. Think about this. How can anyone else forgive you and give you a second chance if you will not give yourself one?

The fourth thing you need to do is ask yourself is, "Did I learn my lesson?" That is pretty simple but necessary. In fact, it is imperative. Okay, you blew it. You hurt someone. You sinned. Now you are in the process of getting better. You are on a journey toward a discovery of a better part of yourself. To do this the right way, you need to ask yourself if you learned your lesson. There is a lot you can learn about yourself in the ashes of a disastrous situation. Take some time to reflect on the path to bad decisions and consider the ways other people's lives have been significantly altered by you. It is a humbling experience but learn from it. Some people are too quick to move on without spending hours, days, weeks, months, even longer reflecting on lessons learned from bad situations of your making.

It is important to learn some things because you should never set out to make the same mistake twice because if you do, maybe you have not learned your lesson in the first place. God did not forgive you so you could go back and do it again. Forgiveness is not an excuse for our actions but it is a second chance to move beyond mistakes and write a new chapter in life.

Fifth, I would encourage you to resist the tendency to isolate yourself and to get some support from other people.

You cannot deal with painful episodes in life and overcome pain that you caused others by yourself. You need a support system. I recommend drawing on your family for support and your faith family. Your family knows you. They know the good, the bad, and the ugly. At this point in your life, there really is no need to try to hide who you are and what you have done. They may be hurt by your actions but they love you and will support your commitment to deal with your actions and change. The saints at the local church are not perfect but they can provide a place where you can be honest about your sins. Most Christians believe in confessing sins and asking God for forgiveness. This simple practice is powerful. It can lift some of the weight of condemnation off your shoulders. Churches are also places you can receive pastoral counsel and preaching that can help you rebuild and redirect your life. You cannot make this journey by yourself. There will be days you feel overwhelmed by the sheer enormity of the situation. That is why family and church members are important. They can encourage you.

The moral of this chapter is to encourage those who fall into sin to face what they have done in a mature manner and responsibly move on with your life. Like Jesus told the woman whose adultery He had forgiven, "go and sin no more lest a worse thing come upon you (John 8:11)." Do not take this second chance as a strike two, thinking I still have one left. If you have truly learned your lesson, you will live like it. Think about it. If you barely recovered from the last trauma, what makes you think you can survive another one like it again? But you should use this second chance like a second birth. Life is new again. Do things right this time.

In conclusion, you should also want to make things right. One of the signs that you have learned your lesson and really changed is to do your best to make things right. When Jesus went to the house of Zacchaeus he stood up and said this. "Behold, Lord, half of my goods I will give to the poor and if I have defrauded anyone of anything, I will give back four times as much. And Jesus said to him, today salvation has come to this house (Luke 19:8-9)." What is so compelling by what Zacchaeus said to Jesus was that no one asked him to do this. He willingly decided to pay back four times as much to anyone he had defrauded. This is compelling in that he willingly decided to do it and he chose to be generous. I believe Zacchaeus has something to teach people who hurt others.

Sometimes people who hurt others are quick in trying move on but do not understand the importance of making things right if it is possible to do so. If you have hurt someone you should try to make it up in some form or another. It may not be possible to make restitution directly. If not, then find another way to be a blessing to someone and to be an agent of healing. Advocate for just and worthy causes, not because you have a guilty conscience, but because you've been forgiven and healed. One thing you could do is to participate in local community support groups and also through the ministry of Jesus Christ through the local church. Find appropriate avenues to share your experiences and wisdom with others in order to keep them from going down the same road you went. Give back to the community, help the needy, and visit the elderly. You would be surprised how much that will help you come to grips with what you did years ago. At least you will have the peace of knowing that you have become a better person. And that is very important. You owe it to yourself and to the one or ones you hurt to turn this pain into good for others. So then, at least, their pain was not totally in vain.

CHAPTER FOUR

LIVING WITH GHOSTS

What was that? So echoes the sentiments of a person who just thought they saw something that was not supposed to be there, something like a ghost. We have all watched a few scary movies in our time. Haunted houses and haunted dreams have been the subject of many thrilling movies. But I want to address the reality of people's lives that seem to be haunted by a painful past. The dictionary defines haunt as to visit often, to come to mind continually, or to be continually present. A painful or sinful past can haunt a person for the rest of their life. People in pain remember the pain, the bad decisions and the dreadful consequences that ensued. Their lives and memories seem to be haunted by the ghosts of mistakes past. That is why I entitled this chapter "Living with Ghosts."

I know it sounds strange but a lot of people live with ghosts. They continually visit the memories and thoughts in dark moments in life. They show up at the worst of times. Ghosts appear at happy occasions trying to steal your joy. Ghosts appear in quiet moments when it is just you and your thoughts. They always seem to catch you off guard. These ghosts have an evil purpose. They try to keep your attention and energy focused on the past instead of the present. Many productive people are hindered by ghosts of mistakes past. Let us explore how this works in the lives of people experiencing pain.

Memories are one of the wonderful and yet mysterious aspects of the human soul. The mind's ability to remember is an essential aspect of human existence. It enhances learning, relationships and personal development. Being able to remember all the good times of the past is an integral part of human life. Precious memories of family gatherings, past holidays, personal accomplishments and lasting friendships all add a sweet savor to life that bring smiles and warm feelings to mind. It is a truly wonderful thing to be able to remember life's experiences.

But there is more to memory than good times. The blessing of memory can also seem like a curse when some are stained with pain. Failure and disappointment in life cannot be forgotten. This is where the ghosts play such a major role in hindering your destiny. While many refer to their precious memories, the hurting are haunted by the pain and failures of yesterday. It is bad enough to have been hurt or to fail at something. The hard part is that our minds will not let us forget our pain. In fact, these ghosts do a good job of keeping these painful memories at the forefront of the mind.

If you have never experienced this you cannot imagine how difficult this can be on a person. All the while going through the normal activities of daily life, ghosts of mistakes and pain past haunt their thoughts. They distract and preoccupy people. They oppress and bombard thoughts.

That is why people struggling with past pain do not recover. It is like their minds will not let them move on. They are living with ghosts. If their thoughts run deep enough, they will surface and resurface. Remember that haunt means to visit often. And that is what these memories do. So the memory as wonderful as it is can also be a two-edged sword as it recalls painful experiences and chapters of your life that you would like to forget. If you are going to recover from the pain of the past you are going to have to learn how to live with the memories but without the ghosts.

I have been talking about ghosts in a metaphorical way but there is a spiritual truth to this. As children of God, we must always remember that we are in a spiritual war and we have an adversary who sincerely desires our destruction. This spiritual war is very real and affects our lives in various ways. For example, the Bible refers to the devil in the book of Revelation as the accuser of the brethren. This title illustrates an important dimension of his work. In the biblical books of Job and Revelation, one of the primary functions of the devil is to accuse people or indict them for the wrong they have done. In the book of Job, Satan wanted to God to allow him to inflict pain on him because he believed Job would curse God. And it seemed like Satan would enjoy rubbing this in God's face. If the devil accuses God's people of wrong before God, I suspect this work takes on another form as it relates to our lives as Christians.

A good place to see this at work is in Paul's second letter to the church at Corinth. Someone in the church had sinned and was dealt with rather sternly. It is possible that this is the person Paul mentioned in 1 Corinthians 5. This man had been involved in a sexual relationship with his father's wife and seemed unrepentant about the situation. Worse yet, the church did nothing about it. Paul scolded them for boasting or kidding around about the situation. So as to draw a clear line that such behavior should not be condoned in the church, Paul told the Corinthians to expel this person (1 Corinthians 5:13). Afterwards Paul writes another letter to the Corinthians and it appears that they did this and the man was repentant. He wanted this man to turn not only from the sin he committed but also from the pain he brought on his family, the church and himself. Paul's advice in the opening part of his second letter was that the Corinthian church should welcome him back. And it is here that he links condemnation to the devices or schemes of Satan.

> But if any have caused grief, he hath not grieved me, but in part: that I may not overcharge you all. Sufficient to such a man is this punishment, which was inflicted of many. So that contrariwise ye ought rather to forgive him, and comfort him, lest perhaps such a one should be swallowed up with overmuch sorrow. Wherefore I beseech you that ye would confirm your love toward him. For to this end also did I write, that I might know the proof of you, whether ye be obedient in all things. To whom ye forgive anything, I forgive also: for if I forgave anything, to whom I forgave it, for your sakes forgave I it in the person of Christ; Lest Satan should get an advantage of us: for we are not ignorant of his devices. (2 Corinthians 2:5-11)

Paul's instructions to the church to forgive, comfort and confirm their love for this person are important not only because they provide a model in how to deal with people who sin and make mistakes. They are important because it reveals what happens when believers are not nurtured through seasons of error. Satan works on weak people who have been isolated because of sin and pain. If stronger believers do not love and comfort and guide weaker believers then Satan gains an advantage. And that is the last thing a destroyer like Satan needs.

When we hear that the devil wants to destroy us we have to understand that he does this in the realm of our minds, the realm of human relationships and in the realm of our situations. Through these avenues, he tries to tempt us to sin which bring harm, defeat and ultimately pain into our lives. In other words, he tempts us to ultimately hurt ourselves because he cannot directly do it himself. One of his major devices is condemnation and he uses real spirits to do this work. The devil not only seeks to entice us to sin but seeks to rub our face in our sin once we commit or give in to temptation. He will use his demons, who are evil spirits, to keep Christians who have been forgiven by God living under condemnation. In other words, the devil harasses and badgers believers until they first ignore and then eventually forget that they are forgiven. So they live like they are under condemnation and judgment. I sincerely believe the devil uses demons to continually accuse and try to bring up past sins in order to immobilize people in pain into living a life of shame, regret and fear. It is a very powerful device of the enemy.

In fact, this device is so powerful that it keeps many believers locked in cycles of defeat. I say this because a person cannot go forward and backwards at the same time. If the devil can keep you focused on what is behind you, you cannot expel all your energy in moving toward your destiny. So he will beat you down with your sin and pain all to keep you from fulfilling your purpose in life, a purpose that goes beyond the sin and mistakes of your past and present. So you must realize that these so-called ghosts are just devices of the devil. And let me tell you something, the devil has destroyed many lives this way. So an important question is "how do you move beyond the haunting effects of these thoughts?" The first step begins with yourself or I should say "within" yourself.

The Struggle of the Soul

There is more to the idea of living with ghosts than memories and Satan's attempt to keep you living in condemnation. One has to look at what happens within the soul of a person who has experienced pain in life. There is a deeply personal aspect to this because some ghosts live within. They abide in the soul and cause us to wrestle within ourselves. Again, I am talking about ghosts in a metaphorical way to speak to the internal struggle of life that is partially a product of life experiences.

When you are dealing with pain in life, you must prepare yourself for one of life's most difficult fights. I am not referring to a physical fight but the fight within one's soul. Some people refer to this fight as the "dark night of the soul" while others refer to it as facing with your "inner demons." These colloquial expressions speak of the struggle within the soul. The darkest nights of the soul are the seasons in life where we wrestle furiously with ourselves. They are times when we are unsure of ourselves and the right path to take and whether we have what it takes to get there. What you will find is that the longer you live the more you will realize that your biggest opponent in life is yourself. While it is always easier to blame others for your life and pain, as you grow in life you will realize just how much you are responsible for the situations you are in and that you have to deal with yourself if you are going to grow and experience healing. At the end of the day, your biggest battle will be within yourself as your struggle with your soul amidst all that life brings you.

Humans are very complex beings that evolve in a variety of ways. For example, from a moral standpoint, people are not good or bad. Rather, humans are a complex combination of good and bad. Within one's soul, there is good and evil. Some people draw on the good that is within more than the bad while others do the opposite and allow evil or sin to be the dominant influence on their lives. You can see what predominates in a person's life from their actions and lifestyles. Jesus describes this principle like this, "wherefore by their fruits ye shall know them" (Matthew 7:20). While this is true, it is equally important to understand that no one is absent of evil desires, motivations and impulses. It is a part of being human and it is even a part of being a Christian. Paul introduced a term in Galatians and Romans that gives language to the principle I am talking about and that term is the flesh. For Paul, the flesh is a term that describes inner desires, motivations and impulses that are sinful. For example, look at this passage in his letter to the Galatians.

> This I say then, walk in the Spirit and ye shall not fulfil the lust of the flesh. For the flesh lusteth against the Spirit, and the Spirit against the flesh; and these are contrary the one to the other; so that ye cannot do the things that ye would (Galatians 5:16-17).

I want to make three points about this Pauline concept. First, Paul instructed in both letters that the counter to the flesh is the Spirit. The flesh and Spirit serve as symbols of a deeper reality within people. The flesh is a symbol of sinful desires and lifestyles. The Spirit represents godly impulses and desires. Second, Paul argued that both the flesh and Spirit manifest negative and positive things in life. For example, in Romans 8, Paul taught that if a person lives by the flesh they will die. In other words, the flesh manifests death. On the other hand, if a person lives in the Spirit they will live. The above text in Galatians pits the flesh against the Spirit. Paul said, they are "contrary one to another." In other words, there is an inner battle between good and evil that Christians live with every single day. Third, Paul exhorts believers to walk in the Spirit and be filled with the Spirit (Galatians 5:25 and Ephesians 5:18). This means that one allows the Holy Spirit to be the dominant and controlling influence. When a person walks in the Spirit, they allow God's power to guide their lifestyle and way of responding to life's challenges.

Paul's ideas about the flesh and the Spirit illumine our inner nature and the challenges of life in helpful ways. In every circumstance and situation in life, we wrestle within ourselves whether to do good or evil. Should I retaliate to the person who just insulted me? Should I forgive my friend who just did something hurtful? Should I give to the church or spend the money on a new outfit? These are just a few examples of daily situations that lay before us choices to either draw on the good within or the impulse to sin. I wanted to lift this idea up because it illustrates what I am talking about here.

Paul's idea about the flesh helps us to see the dual and conflicting aspects of good and evil in the soul. It also helps us to understand why we behave in good ways and evil ways in different aspects of their lives. The truth is we are walking contradictions of good and evil, generosity and selfishness, love and hatred, kindness and indifference, etc. A person can be a racist to people who are different and yet a loving father to his children. In both relationships they tap into their capacity for good and evil. Humans can be that contradictory. You are contradictory. I am contradictory. I want you to do something for me. Put this book down and go to a mirror and take a long look into your eyes. Look at yourself and think about what we've just learned. Look at yourself and think of the myriad of ways you embody the best and worst of you. You may even want to write some thoughts down on a piece of paper as you think about the complex impulses and desires that make you- YOU.

In a sense, life is about dealing with YOU- the better parts of you and the worse parts of you. Growth and healing and success in life depends on how we balance and address good and evil impulses in the soul. There are impulses and desires within the soul that inspire us to be our best selves. Love others. Be kind to those who dislike and mistreat you. Forgive people for hurting you. Do not speak evil of other people because they are children of God, too. Be generous even though you may not be appreciated for it. Admit wrongs and ask for forgiveness. However, there are impulses and desires within the soul that want to draw on the worst part of us. Get revenge for what someone did to you. Do not forgive that person who hurt you. Laugh at someone's misfortune. Ignore the suffering of others. There is not a person alive that does not live with both impulses and desires and draw on them in a variety of ways. That is why people are walking contradictions of good and evil, love and hate, etc. That is why we behave in duplicitous ways leading people to believe that we are hypocrites. It is because life is an ongoing struggle with the soul.

I said all this to get to make a very important point. Not only do we have these impulses and desires, we have acted upon them and they have caused others pain and even brought pain on ourselves. And it is hard to live with the realization of what we are capable of depending on circumstances and our state of mind. That is the part of living with ghosts that I want to address. A lot of people live in denial of the things they have done to hurt others and themselves. They blame others. But they know within themselves what they have done and that within their soul there is the same impulse and desire for evil and sin. So what should we do?

We have to accept ourselves. If we do not learn how to accept ourselves as beings with the dual capacity for good and evil, then we will live the rest of our lives struggling with deep-seated feelings of insecurity that are rooted in self-doubt and fear. When we do not accept the better parts and the worse parts, we doubt ourselves constantly thinking "I might do it again so it is better not to do anything." When we do not accept ourselves, we are afraid that the future may be a repeat of the past. Every time we have an opportunity to move forward, we fight intensely personal and painful battles in our souls over whether we should even try. By not accepting ourselves, we only prolong the dark nights of the soul. We leave ourselves ever second-guessing ourselves and never giving ourselves space to be imperfect and to grow.

If we are going to grow and experience healing, we have to face who we are and what we wrestle with as children of God. I refer to this as the process of facing and accepting the darkness within the soul. We have to face our inner ghosts and demons. Many of us live with deep doubts and fears about ourselves and the reason for doubts and fears are connected to impulses and desires within that we deny are there in the first place. There is a better way to live. A part of healing requires brutal self-honesty. You must have the courage to tell yourself the truth and to accept yourself as an imperfect person. Instead of denying who you are, accept who you are. Face it but do not let sinful impulses and desires be the controlling influence of life. Live a life where the Spirit leads you and helps you with impulses that will hurt others and ultimately yourself. Second, we must find peace. Healing is about being at peace with yourself and while it does not come instantly, peace does come. That means, you have accepted all aspects of yourself and the path you took to get where you are today. Once you do this, you can hold your head up in life because you are at peace in your soul.

Hold Your Head Up

Good advice- but is it that easy? When you have to recover from some of the difficulties of the past holding your head up is not as easy as some would like it to be. When you have to live with the ghosts of your past every time you feel like holding your head up or sticking your chest out, they remind you of the pain of life experiences gone bad. Instead of praying for you and offering thoughtful encouragement, many Christians are content to blurt out a saying that is supposed to solve all your problems. Little do they know that you are living with ghosts. This very common scenario reminds me of Jesus' parable on prayer in Luke 18.

> The Pharisee stood and prayed thus with himself, God I thank thee that I am not as other men are, extortioners, unjust, adulterers, or even as this publican. I fast twice in the week, I give tithes of all that I possess. And the publican standing afar off, would not lift up so much as his eyes to heaven, but smote his breast, saying, God be merciful to me a sinner (Luke 18:11-14).

The Pharisee reminds me of some Christians who have not been through anything. Their testimony is that they are better off than most people because they have not done this or that. They are certainly not as bad as the sinners they love pointing out to God and others. It must be real nice to have that testimony. Some people in life got the breaks and made the right decisions. They dotted their "I's" and crossed their "T's." However there are those in church who are like the publican. They have not made all the right decisions. In fact, they dotted their "T's" and crossed their "I's." And there is a growing segment of our society and also in the church of people who fit this description. Their lives are not a pretty picture. Like the publican, they feel that they have no right to even lift their heads to heaven. Sin and pain have beaten them down so they only ask for God's mercy. You see, when you have been through the depths of sin and pain holding your head up is very difficult.

It is very difficult because the ghosts of your past remind you of where you came from. The rest of your life then becomes a paradox of mixed interests. Let me explain. When you have sinned, part of the consequences for sinning is not being able to forget what transpired and how it affected people. This is a part of the therapy of sin and God's way of deterring you from repeating past sins. So I do not care how many times people tell you that your sin is behind you, it will never be absent from your memory. I know this sounds strange but you should remember your sins. However, you should not let your past sins control you or dictate your future. That is part of the paradox. You live with the memory of your sin but have been forgiven for the act so you can move forward. There is a verse in Philippians that explains how to live in light of this paradox.

> Brethren I count not myself to have apprehended; but this one thing I do, forgetting those things which are behind,

and reaching forth unto the things which
are before. I press towards the mark for the
prize of the high calling of God in Christ
Jesus (Philippians 3:14).

Paul is instructing that there are some things that you
are going to have to put behind you if you are going to reach
your mark in life. However, it is clear from other scriptures
that Paul did not forget his past sins.

And I thank Christ Jesus our Lord, who
hath enabled me for that he counted me
faithful, putting me into the ministry; who
was before a blasphemer, and persecutor,
and injurious: but I obtained mercy (1
Timothy 1:12-13).

For I am the least of the apostles, that I
am not meet to be called an apostle,
because I persecuted the church of God (1
Corinthians 15:9).

Paul continually lamented his past behavior towards the
church that he so lovingly served after his road to Damascus
experience. He also marveled at the grace of God in that
he could be totally forgiven and used as an apostle of Jesus
Christ. Do you see the paradox? You put some things behind
you, then you press forward, but you never forget. So you
can hold your head up because of God's grace all the while
feeling the sentiments of that publican who knows that he
has no right to do so.

Now please understand me, I am not advocating a guilt ridden lifestyle or living under the condemnation that Jesus died for us to be free from. The guilt of sin has been completely removed by the precious blood of Jesus. However the Bible is equally clear that the presence of sin has not been done away with. So that means that we live in a hurting world where the possibility of sin and suffering exist. And how we handle our sin says everything about our faith in God.

The Power of Prayer and Confession

> Confess your faults one to another that ye may be healed, and pray for one that ye may be healed. The effectual fervent prayer of a righteous man availeth much (James 5:16).

If prayer and confession of sin are necessary aspects of healing or wholeness, then sin has to take something from you. When you sin, believe it or not, you lose something. Romans 6:15-23 reveals that sin enslaves and its penalty is death. So it is clear that God has set up a way so that sin has a price. You lose something when you go beyond God's will for your life. And that loss is why prayer and confession are so therapeutic. You see, only God through the love of Christ and presence of the Holy Spirit can restore to you what sin took away.

I consider prayer and confession as spiritual rehabilitation. It takes this to recover from what sin has done to you and also what you have done to yourself. Prayer and confession not only invites the Lord's assistance, it invites the love and support of other Christians. Getting over what you have lost can be a reality with other Christians praying for you and with you. They are also there to listen to your struggles and anything else that you feel you need to get off your chest.

Conclusion

You do not have to let your thoughts hold you hostage. There is not anything you can do about what happened in your past. It is over. I know it does not seem like it when you close your eyes and see the people who hurt you or the people you hurt or when you almost relive it in the deep recesses of the mind. You have to settle it in your mind and heart- it is over. Tell yourself that it's over. Tell yourself that that chapter of your life has ended and you are re-writing how the next one will end. Then tell the devil to shut up. God has forgiven you so it really does not matter what he says. Use those painful thoughts as motivation for personal improvement. What does not kill you makes you stronger. So when those thoughts come up, praise God for his wonderful mercy and grace. Thank him for the second or third, or even tenth chance that he has so graciously given you. Finally, decide to move on with your life.

PART II

WHAT TO DO ABOUT THE PAIN

What makes pain so difficult to cope with is the shock that you have been hurt. Everyone knows that people get hurt but we are invariably caught off guard when it actually happens to us. We tend to think of those things happening to someone else. One of the most important aspects of recovering from pain is accepting the reality that is has happened to you. Either you have been hurt or have caused pain for someone else. You have to accept this. It is not television. It is personal. It has hit home. It has happened to you. Now what are you going to do about it? I will tell what to do. You take life one day at a time and make your mind up that your life is not over. After that, you begin the journey of dealing with the pain.

CHAPTER FIVE

DECISIONS DECISIONS DECISIONS

So many times, when life seems unfair or when we are hurting, we ask ourselves how did we get here? I cannot count the times I have asked myself that question. Well the truth is if you look back and really think about things you will find that a bad decision or a series of bad decisions may be the reason why you are in the situation that is hurting you. The easy thing to do is to find someone to blame. To some extent our society encourages us to blame others and rarely look at ourselves. Many love to blame either someone they love for letting them down or they blame God. There are also people who blame their family or social environment and society for their pain. There are times when the decisions of others, particularly those with power and influence, can affect your life. In those instances, there is not a thing you can do to prevent them from doing something to bring hurt and pain to your life. It is important to talk about decision-making at this level because it acknowledges systemic dimension to life and its effect on people's lives. But that is not the only way to talk about decision-making. I want to focus on an individual's freedom and ability to make decisions that affect their lives because people need to understand how decisions can help them deal with their pain. So I turn to this task now.

Situational pain is often a result of bad choices. In a given situation or circumstance, every person has the freedom to choose how they are going to respond. A bad decision can bring pain into your life and you have no one to blame but yourself. After all, you chose this path. This may be the most important thing you will ever read in your entire life. One bad decision or a series of bad decisions can change the landscape of your entire life. The changes that result from a bad decision are very real and very painful. Your life can be affected by your bad decisions. This is a challenging concept to really think through and an even greater responsibility given to us by God. Our decisions do matter and have a significant impact on our lives as well as the lives of others. Therefore, the issue of decision-making is very serious and the first place to really begin the journey toward healing.

The Basics of Life and Decisions

Life is often defined life as the physical, mental, and spiritual experiences that constitute a person's existence. With this basic definition in mind, one could say life is the combined experiences or events of life that transpire over the course of a given number of years. God gives us life- and years, months, weeks, days, hours, minutes, and seconds measure this life. The totality of experiences or events is your life. However, there is more to life than just the years, months, weeks, days, hours and minutes. There is this idea of the good life. The good life reflects the belief that the majority of one's life is deemed good. There is more good than bad. So people strive for a life where the good outweighs the bad. This is precisely why decisions are important because they play a direct role in the kind of experiences we have in life.

Within the period of time that we call life, decisions directly and indirectly determine the quality of life experiences- whether good or bad. The decisions we make determines the path we take in life. While on a certain path in life, we have certain experiences that lead to life happiness and worth. Thus decisions dictate whether a person experiences life satisfaction or life dissatisfaction because good experiences in life are a result of good decisions and bad experiences in life are a result of a bad decision on your behalf or someone else's behalf. There is a direct correlation one to the other. The more good experiences one has in life the higher their quality of life will be and more likely to have high levels of life satisfaction. The same is true for those who have more bad experiences. Their quality of life seems to be lower and their level of life satisfaction is low. Why is this the case? It is because the decisions we make affect our lives. That is why we have to be very careful about the decisions we make and take this responsibility very seriously.

Life is not to be trifled with or taken lightly. You have a significant role in shaping the trajectory of your life and your destiny. Nevertheless, you must choose wisely because there are multiple destinations, both good and bad.

> See I have set before thee this day life and
> good, and death and evil…I call heaven and
> earth to record this day against you that I
> have set before you life and death, blessing
> and cursing; therefore choose life, that both
> thou and thy seed may live (Deuteronomy
> 30:15, 19).

So as you either look ahead to the years that are before
you or look back over the years that have transpired, please
realize the important role decision-making has played in
your life. One of the reasons decision-making is not taken
as seriously as it should be is because it is a part of daily
life. Daily responsibilities are the easiest things to take for
granted. I say this because people tend to just get caught up
in going through the motions instead of paying attention
and giving care to the things that need it. I believe this to
be the number one enemy to relationships and genuine
lively religion. People have a tendency to grow complacent
and get used to the things that are closest to them. This
is such a great enemy because it causes so many people to
lose sight of the big picture. That is actually what makes
daily events so significant. They are small integral parts of
a much larger and important picture. For example, a golden
wedding anniversary is the culmination of two persons who
took love one day at a time until they turned around and
realized that 18, 250 days had transpired. Each day of loving
one another played an important part for that couple to
experience a golden wedding anniversary. The same is also
true for those who end up going to hell. So many of them
fail to realize the daily opportunities they had to glorify God

and serve him. They neglected the daily aspects of faith that in turn results in a lifestyle of unbelief that is ultimately punished by God.

> So teach us to number our days that we may apply our hearts unto wisdom (Psalm 90:12).

Every day we face circumstances and situations that we have to decide in what way to respond. And if we are not careful to make wise decisions, we minimize the importance of the particular decision at hand. When we do this we tend to make decisions that are shortsighted. What I mean by that is the decision is good for now but may not be what is best in the long run. A series of decisions like this can set you on a path that will eventually lower your quality of life and level of life satisfaction.

People today are in love with the moment. Instant gratification is the way so many of us take when it comes to decision-making. But this is the worst way to live your life especially when it comes to making important decisions. When we live for the moment we live foolishly. So also when we make decisions based on instant gratification we make foolish decisions. And these decisions lead to difficult situations and more pain. So much evil in our world is a direct result of people who live for the nasty now. Violence, sexual immorality, financial irresponsibility and familial hardships are all directly or indirectly related to decisions made in a shortsighted manner. You always make better decisions when you do what is best in the long run.

That is why the above Scripture is so powerful. We need to be instructed to number our days. I believe that what the Psalmist is really getting at is valuing our days. When we value our days, we place a premium on the decisions that those days present us. Maybe you are reading this and feel that you need to make better decisions. Numbering your days can help. It puts you in the position to direct your life in a certain way that greatly increases quality of life.

Numbering our days is a very interesting concept. Did you know that a person on their 20th birthday has lived approximately 7300 days; a person on their 40th birthday has lived approximately 14,600 days, while a person on their 70th birthday has lived approximately 25,550 days? Now discounting their childhood, what have they done with this time, with each and every day? What have you done? Maybe you need to begin numbering your days. Because when you do number your days you position yourself to use each day in a wise manner. In other words, you realize how each day can be used to direct you to your destiny. So one day at a time you make individual decisions that help you to go in that direction. Then over the course of time you find yourself in a good position. This is the lifestyle that leads to life satisfaction.

> Trust in the Lord with all thine heart and lean not unto thine own understanding. In all thy ways acknowledge Him, and He shall direct thy paths (Proverbs 3:5-6).

The thought that your destiny is up to your ability to make good decisions is daunting. However, you are not on your own. God is there to help lead us and guide us through all that life may present us. Jesus at his first coming was referred to as Emmanuel, which means "God with us." This title for Christ is indicative of the truth that God is with his people. So we do not have to fear that the onus is entirely on us. The above text reminds us that we are to trust in the Lord. In other words, we need to depend on God's power and ability to help us and not our own understanding. We cannot do everything right but God specializes in helping the weak. Whatever weakness we have, God makes up for it when we trust in him. This is such good news. If I rely and depend on God's power and wisdom, the Scripture tells me that He will direct my paths. Please remember this because it is the capstone of the decision making issue. Having God's help is the greatest way to realizing life satisfaction.

> The steps of a good man are ordered by the Lord and he delighteth in his way. Though he fall he shall not be utterly cast down; for the Lord upholdeth him with his hand (Psalm 37:23-24).

This verse reminds us of the wonderful truth that God guides his children even when they make mistakes. Trusting in the Lord's leading is the best way. It insures that though you may stumble, God will help keep you on the right path. In boxing, this would be the difference between being knocked down and being knocked out. God's help prevents knock- outs. God always providentially works in the circumstances of his people to bring about good for them. Paul reminds us of this in the book of Romans.

> And we know that all things work together
> for good to them that love God, to them,
> who are the called according to his purpose
> (Romans 8:28).

God is faithful through all our circumstances to bring out good for his people. Now let me say that God has the right to decide what is good for us. Sometimes the things that we call bad are used by God to benefit us in the long run. So do not just limit this verse to imply that God always plans happy times for his children. God brings about good, not ease.

Making Decisions while Hurting

Before I conclude this chapter, I want to share a word of caution and a few words of wisdom about the challenges of making good decisions when you are hurting. I remember when I was a young pastor. I was twenty-one years old and thought I had the world and life all figured out. One day, I was talking with a few deacons at the church and was feeling particularly inspired so I opened my mouth and said this, "Don't ever make a major decision in a storm." I went on to explain that in storms and difficult moments in life we tend to make rushed and rash decisions. I said it is always best to wait until the storm is over before making a major decision. In hindsight I can see the wisdom in what I was saying and there is a considerable degree of truth in it but as I have matured I realize life does not always give you the opportunity to delay a decision because it is a bad time for you. The truth of the matter is that life does not stop because you are hurting. If it is possible to delay making major decision when you are in pain, I would encourage you to do so. It is always a good practice to carefully think on things and pray before deciding what to do. But there are times you have to make important decisions while in pain. You may have family and work responsibilities that require your attention and resultant decisions. So I want to offer some guidance in how to do this.

First, I want you to be aware of yourself and your feelings because feelings influence your state of mind and mood, both of which complicate the decision-making process. Learning to identify and name feelings can be very helpful. You may want to write them down in a journal. This is important because it allows you to take a step back and gain some perspective on the situation requiring a decision. And the more perspective you gain the better decision you are likely to make. Being mindful and aware of your feelings, some of which may be in conflict with each other, can help slow your thought processes down enough to think clearly. I say that because when you are hurting, natural instincts will want to kick in. While there are some benefits to natural instincts there are considerable disadvantages. Instinct will work in ways that try to address the immediate need of the hurt. For some reason, we are hard wired to focus on what's ailing us and hurting, even if there are hundred great things going on in our lives. Our instinct is to focus on the pain and alleviate it.

This instinct gets us in trouble sometimes because we are so focused on stopping the pain that in our condition of vulnerability we turn to things that provide temporary relief. And the truth is many things that provide temporal relief only make matters worse and further complicate your situation. When you allow pain to consume your mental energies, it will push you to do something to alleviate it. This is what leads to rushed, rash and reckless decisions. Learning to be mindful of your feelings is a helpful counter to these instincts and learned behaviors. Name those feelings. Identify those feelings. Sit with those feelings. But do not allow feelings to function as the rudder of your ship. The word of God, your values, and good counsel should do that. Feelings of anxiety, fear and jealousy will cause you to make bad decisions. Learn how to practice patience. Teach yourself to sit with feelings, even negative ones and not allow those feelings to push you to do anything. Because it is in the process of sitting with those feelings that God can bring clarity of mind and peace, which results in better decisions.

Second, the next major challenge to making decision when hurting results from dealing with uncertainty. All decisions are characterized by some degree of incertitude. Humans are finite beings. We do not know the future. We have no idea how things will turn out after a decision. It is both humbling and important to accept one's finitude. Human decisions are always contingent on the reality of our complete ignorance of the outcome. But when you are hurting there is an additional layer that complicates the decision process. People in pain are unsure of themselves. It kind of goes with the territory. Their bad decisions could have contributed to their pain. It could also have been their decision to trust their lives to a person who hurt them. Either way they are in pain and sometimes it increases self-doubt significantly. The reality of their pain causes them to turn inward and question and blame themselves. And the greater the level of self-doubt the less likely the person will trust themselves to make good decisions in the present.

This is why it is absolutely critical to do two these two things on an on-going basis. First, practice self-forgiveness. Learn to forgive others and by all means, learn to forgive yourself for being finite, imperfect and in process. Otherwise you will find yourself refusing to make decisions for yourself or worse yet abdicating that responsibility to someone else. Like I said earlier, life does not always wait for a better time for a decision. There are times you have to make a decision and you should go ahead and make the decision. Second, get comfortable with mixed feelings. Once you have named and identified your feelings, it helps you deal with the ways you feel divided about the proper course of action. The hardest decisions in life are the ones you feel divided about. You see equal advantages and disadvantages. You see an equal amount of strengths and weaknesses. You see opportunities and perils. And it is hard to decide which course of action or path to take. Again, mindfulness of mixed feelings is a good thing. It is a good place to begin, just do not stay there too long. One can only analyze feelings for so long before a decision is needed. It is here that one should turn to God for wisdom.

> If any of you lack wisdom, let him ask of God that gives to all liberally and unbraids not; and it shall be given to them. But let one ask in faith, nothing wavering. For the one who wavering is like a wave of the sea driven with the wind and tossed. For let not that one think he or she shall receive

anything from the Lord. A double-minded
person is unstable in all ways (James 1:5-8).

Asking God for wisdom may seem simplistic but is actually the best next step to take after mindfulness because it keeps you from the trap of double-mindedness or duplicity. Being of two minds for extended periods in life is not good. The Scripture in James 1 calls such a person unstable and promises that they will not receive anything from God. Wisdom comes in many forms. God gives wisdom through counsel from mature and responsible believers. God gives wisdom in the form of personal illumination and insight through prayer and meditation. God gives wisdom through sermons and teachings from Scripture. Ask God in faith and move in faith. That is how divine wisdom touches and guides finite persons who are uncertain about a decision. If God wanted us to make perfect decisions, He would have given us all knowledge. Since we lack that, then we rely on Him to the best of our ability and make a decision.

In conclusion, if you want your life to be good again, and want to escape the pain of the past, then start making better decisions. And you cannot make better decisions if you are not serious about them and are not prepared for this great responsibility. All you have to do is embrace the challenge of making good decisions, then commit your life to God so he can help you. For example, ask yourself these three questions, "What decision or series of decisions contributed to the pain I am experiencing?" "What is my role in my pain?" "What can I do to change how I make decisions?" Answering questions like these can be a helpful beginning point that leads to lasting change and moral growth. That is how you get on the right track to life satisfaction. But living for the moment or just making decisions as they come without considering the big picture is not wise. Please be careful about the decisions you make.

CHAPTER SIX

THE ROAD TO HEALING

A new journey in life begins with one step. But when you are hurting one step can seem impossible. I have been there. I have had days when a single step seemed impossible. I wanted to sit down or lay down and not make another move forward. It is ok. There are dark days in life. I want to be totally transparent here and not sugar coat the difficult nature of healing from pain. It is a long hard road but I can testify that it is well worth it because God is so faithful and present in tough times. Before I discuss this road to healing, I want to emphasize the importance of surviving difficult moments in life before these nights precede mornings when things look and feel better.

Getting through Dark Nights

I want to keep it real. To a certain extent, healing slowly manifests and a person recovers from past pain incrementally. There are good days and there are bad days. And the bad days can be very bad. In fact, my favorite description for bad days is the metaphor of "dark nights." The Bible talks about this experience in different ways. Psalm 23 refers to it as the "valley and shadow of death." Psalm 40 describes it as a "horrible pit" and Psalm 91 calls it "the terror by night." In the New Testament, Jesus had a very dark night in the Garden of Gethsemane. He confessed to his disciples that his "soul is exceeding sorrowful even unto death" (Matthew 26). Paul characterized his dark night as being "pressed out of measure, above strength, insomuch that he despaired of life" (2 Corinthians 1). This rich language and imagery in Scripture gives witness to moments in life that are so difficult that it feels like death is approaching. There are days that seem very dark. During dark nights you wrestle with hopelessness. During dark nights, you struggle with self-doubt. You doubt God and others. Dark nights cause crippling fear and dread that can immobilize you. Some nights you feel the full weight of your situation and it overwhelms you. Some nights can be so dark that you despair of life. Suicidal ideation may emerge because the pain can be so intense. And sadly, some turn to suicide during these very dark nights.

Here is the real truth. There will be dark nights. It is inevitable. There will be days when your pain will make you feel like a motherless child. There will be days you may feel like Job when he said "cursed be the day I was born." These days are meant to be survived. I know this goes against the theology of TV preachers who will tell you to flex your spiritual muscles in dark times and never ever doubt or be afraid. But the truth is people in pain have those days and moments. So instead of telling them they need to do this or that, I want to keep it real and say some dark days are meant to be survived. I believe there is something important about drawing on the little strength you have left to live to fight another day. Sometimes surviving is the best thing you can do. Sometimes the sheer will to hold on is often neglected in modern preaching and teaching. I want to lift that up because surviving dark nights says something about a person's faith and strength. Psalm 118:17 says, "I shall not die but live and declare the works of the Lord." In a real way that is exactly what a survivor of dark nights says and believes with everything that is within them. They fight and push to get through the dark until the night ends. So before embarking on this road, I want to nurture the kind of determination that you will need when the night comes.

The Journey to Healing

Let us begin. I wrote this book to challenge you to confront the issues, problems, and pain that life has given you and become a better person. My explanations will be simple but putting them into practice will not be easy. First of all, you have to make up your mind that you are not going to quit. There is an old saying that claims, "Quitters never win and winners never quit." I believe that to be true. There are few things worse than a quitter. Things got tough, things went sour, things were not easy, so they took the easy way out and quit. Let me tell you something. Anybody can give up. Anybody can quit. It is the easy way out. It is the sort of attitude that many persons who quit have. They would rather give up than be committed to seeing a tough situation through. Instead of facing the people they hurt, or facing the situation that is plaguing them, some opt to quit.

The quitters I am referring to are the ones who do not end their lives but who keep on living. They are alive but in their hearts have given up on themselves and the possibility that things can get better. They are difficult people to be around and to help. When many around them are talking about future plans, they are not interested in the future. In their minds, their future is condemned because of their past. They have given up on good future. They have given up on believing in the good life. When I say the good life, I am talking about a life of joy, peace, happiness, love of God, family and friends, relationships and work. Many people, because of past pain, have given up on trying to make sense of life. They have grown weary in trying to get over hurtful situations and are resolved to quit and punish the world for their plight. That is the mindset of the quitter.

Quitters isolate themselves from people. They wallow in self-pity. They want life to stop and wait for them to get over the pain of the past. They want the whole world to apologize to them. They are quitters! There is no possible way to recover or rebuild your life if you have already decided that it is too late. If you have decided to quit, you are in big trouble. As long as there is breath and strength in your body, you have to keep fighting because things can get better. But if you quit, you may never see good days again. Somewhere in your heart is a ray of hope. You have to believe that the sun can and will shine again. Maybe it is going to take some time but your situation is not beyond repair. Things can get better. You have to be determined that you are not going to quit.

Secondly, you have to take your recovery one day at a time. The road to recovery has to be travelled in increments.

I know it sounds old fashioned, but it is true. And I can honestly say that I am not particularly fond of this truth. Sometimes I wish recovery was instant but it is not. Life is made up of days, one after the other. If you just focus on one day you can recover from pain and rebuild your life. Focus on doing things differently for that day and thinking differently for that day and before long you will have months and years behind you. But if you get ahead of yourself and start trying to figure out the future and how long a path you have to recovery you can become overwhelmed. Now is not the time to worry what you are going to be doing in five years or what you are going to do with the rest of your life. Just concentrate on the task at hand which is today. It is within your power to make today better than yesterday. You cannot leap forward a couple of years. All you need to be concerned with is today. Try with all that is within you to get better and make the best of the day at hand. Try to improve your character, decision-making abilities, how you relate to family and friends, job performance and your overall thoughts about life.

If you concentrate on improvement each day, over time things will get better. Now you are going to have some good days and some bad days, but if you take them one at a time, you will get a better handle on the ups and downs of life. Remember that becoming a better person is all you can do. Do not waste your time and energies on what you cannot change. Recovering is like walking. Walking consists of taking single steps over and over again. Recovery will come one day at a time. Just take your time and allow the days, like steps, to get you living the good life again. It is one step, by step, by step. It is one day, two days, three days and then it is months, then years. Do you see how that works?

The most difficult part to accept is that recovery takes time. In a day where microwaves provide instant food, remote controls and satellites give us instant entertainment, and the internet gives us instant access to the world. We like things to happen instantly. But recovery is not something that can be gained quickly. Recovery takes time. It takes time to heal hurt. That's life. But I promise you, things can get better.

Time Machines

Finally if you are going to recover from past pain, you have to understand that you cannot change the past. When you are hurting, you are constantly beating yourself over the head, wishing you could go back in your past and fix things that went wrong. If you are a cartoon fan, like I am, you know about the villains that created a time machine so they could go back and create the past in order to create a world where they are the ultimate ruler of the galaxy or world. The logic says if I can stop the good guys before they get on the scene, then no one will be around to stop me when it is time for me to take over the world. Well the villain never quite got things to work out the way they planned but did indeed pose an interesting concept.

Imagine if a time machine was a real possibility. Imagine how wonderful it would be to go back, correct our mistakes, and fix things before they went bad for us and others. What a wonderful world it would be or would it? When you are hurting, you are constantly beating yourself up wishing you could go back and correct things. The logic here is, "if only I could go back, things would be much different, much better." Sometimes the hurting will exhaust hours of imagination into this. If only I had done this or did not do that or did not meet this person. Now I would to God sometimes that I could to back and fix some things that went wrong in my life, but that is a waste of time because I cannot go back. Why should I waste time thinking about things I would do differently in my past when all I should be concentrating on is learning from the mistakes I have already made? My focus should be on what is within my power to change. Let me repeat myself. It is a waste of time imagining what you would do differently if you could go back. Focus your energies on what you learned from past mistakes, and commit yourself to doing better in the future. That is all you can do. You cannot go back! Get that out of your head. Whether someone has hurt you or you have hurt someone else, you cannot go back and change it.

Time to go to School

Even though school is the epicenter of educational endeavors in our society, learning is not just limited to school. Life can give you an expensive education. We learn by reason, by using our minds in a structured curriculum from kindergarten to high school and even on through college. But, experience teaches us much about life that cannot be limited to a grade. I do not care how knowledgeable you may be with books and university degrees life is going to teach you some things. There is not a person exempt from the education life provides. If you live long enough, you will learn plenty about life. Life is the composite of experiences measured by the amount of years you are alive on this planet. Life is like cake. Cake tastes good, but it takes eggs, flour and other stuff (you can tell I'm not a cook) to make it edible. You cannot leave certain ingredients out because you do not like them individually. Each individual part makes a cake complete and ready to eat. That is the way life is. You have to take the good with the bad. Even though you would like to change the bad, it is part of your experience of life. You have to accept that. You're in school like I'm in school. Everybody makes mistakes that they cannot go back and change. Just accept that this too is a part of your life's education.

Get Real Because Life is not a Fairy Tale

Wouldn't life be grand if we all "lived happily ever after?" Well that is just not the case. I love watching television and movies but in a way they have deceived many people. You see, what goes on in television and the movies are not real. It is for our entertainment. But some people fail to realize that fact. The line between entertainment and real life gets blurred for them. Trends are changing now but it used to be a time when everything always worked out for the best on television. The good guys always won, the family always stayed together and the town ridded itself of evil, etc. Once the line between entertainment and reality got blurred, that kind of message caused people to have an unrealistic perception of life. And people today harbor that same idea that life is a fairy tale with a good ending. The fairy tale attitude that is really unrealistic is that there is a life without mistakes. Humanity as we know it demands that people are going to make mistakes. But it seems that when humanity happens, everybody is in shock as if it is some new trend. People make mistakes. That is a part of life also.

Now let's get real. Life would be a joke if we could always go back and change our past mistakes. That's for Saturday morning cartoons, not real life. How could we ever improve our character if we did not learn from past mistakes? How could any human improve their personal worth if it was not for mistakes showing them there is a better way? A life without consequences, without peaks and valleys, ups and downs is not a life at all; it is a joke, a cartoon. What is real is the school of hard knocks. What is real is whether or not you have the guts to get up after you have fallen and still make something good of your life. What is real is learning from the mistakes of the past. Did you learn your lesson? If so, then move on with your life because that is the best path to take when you've been hurt or hurt someone yourself.

Life is a gift from God. God gives us life and places it within our power to improve our lives and please him, or waste our lives hurting others and giving up on ourselves and all the potential God has given us. It is not a fairy tale or horror story, but a special gift, a slice of eternity called time, an opportunity to do something good or do something worthless. The choice is yours. That is what life is all about. So do not deprive all the ones who love you and need your love, your gift, your contribution to humanity by trying to recreate something that you cannot. You cannot change the past, but you certainly can change your future. Ask yourself, what good does it accomplish by beating yourself up over past failures and what good can you accomplish for anyone if you have not moved beyond your past? Moving forward is the thing to do.

On this journey, there are five areas that I challenge you to address in order to fully walk in the healing that God desires for you. The areas all relate to pain and how best to apply healing to it. Pain affects how we live, how we interact with others, how we view life, how we respond to community and how we respond to God. Let us take a closer look at these areas and find ways to experience healing.

How We Live: Living Hurt or Living Healed

This is arguably the make or break point in the book. Now that you have been hurt, it is your decision as to whether you want to live hurt or live healed. You do have a choice. How many persons have been negatively affected by individuals who have been hurt in the past? These persons have almost stopped living and deprive those they love from a future of happiness. These wounded warriors live in the past. Their progress ceased when they were wounded. So instead of using their pain to better themselves, they allow life to knock them out of contention and thus punish those they love for the pain they cannot overcome. They decide to live hurt rather than live healed. These kinds of persons are the worse parents one can have. They make poor leaders in the church. Anyone is just about useless when they have decided to live hurt. It's difficult to implement visions for the future when you are locked in your past, living out past pain, punishing the world because life has been unfair to you. Living hurt hurts others: parent child relationships, marital relationships, relationships at church, coworkers, etc.

How do you expect to have a good marriage when you treat all men like the one that hurt you or treat all women like the one who hurt you? How can you deal fairly with all people when you view the entire church like your past congregation? In other words, how can you go forward while looking backward? You have to decide whether you are going to live hurt or live healed. This is a decision you have to make. Most people who have been really hurt do not decide to commit suicide, they decide to live but mostly their decision is to live hurt. It's kind of like getting shot in the side and deciding not to go to the hospital for help. You just sort of think that I will live with the wound untreated. Well you don't have to be a medical doctor to know that is a bad decision. And the decision to live hurt without really dealing with that pain is not a wise choice for you or the ones you love.

If you know anything about a wounded animal, you know that once they get hedged in, they will attack. And wounded people are the same way; they attack almost anyone around, many times unknowingly, because they are living hurt. These persons are usually very defensive about almost everything. They tend to think that the world is out to get them. So they react accordingly, scratching and clawing through life and many times at the ones they love. Let me give you some examples of living hurt: not forgiving someone who wronged you, keeping a tragic incident to yourself, instead of opening up and getting help; trying to hate someone for the rest of your life, allowing a past tragedy to destroy your life, isolating yourself from family, friends, church and God, giving up on trying to make the best out of life, and allowing your life to become increasingly immoral trying to cover your pain. None of these things will help you. In fact they will destroy you. You owe it to yourself to decide to live healed and not hurt. Your life matters. You are important. And most of all, people need you.

Interaction with Others: Stop Bleeding On Me

I assure you this is the cry of those who love you. Stop bleeding on me means stop taking your pain out on me. It is a shame that we spend years of our lives punishing the ones we love for something they had nothing to do with. I know their cry is, "will you stop taking your bitterness out on me!" You see, the hurt cannot help themselves. Their condition leads them to punish almost anyone just because they have been hurt. Sadly, most of the time they do not mean to do it. They are just out of control. However, it is no excuse for taking your pain out on those who had absolutely nothing to do with the situation.

Listen to me, if you have been hurt in the past and want to ever enjoy the good life again, you have to stop bleeding on the people you love. You will end up pushing away the ones whom you really need. If you have been hurt, you will make your life more miserable by hurting the ones who really want to help you. Please remember this.

It is vital that you come to a place of spiritual wholeness, so you will stop hurting the people you love. You have to overcome your pain for the benefit of those around you who love you and need you. When your wounds get healed, you can stop bleeding on others and start being an agent of healing for others who have been hurt. Remember the ones who cry "stop bleeding on me"- your future, your family, your friends, the members of the church you attend and your co-workers.

View of Life: Looking Through Pains Lenses

Pain has an uncanny way of rearranging your worldview. It affects the way you view every facet of life and the rearrangement is usually for the worse. A positive worldview turns negative. The belief that life is good turns to "life sucks." Almost every facet of our existence gets affected when we don't get over our pain. Too many view life through the lenses of pain. They see an evil world full of evil people because they have been hurt. Their personal pain shapes their worldview. It is apparent to them that since this world allowed them to be hurt the way they were, it must be evil. In situations where many would see something positive, the person who lives with past pain sees something negative. For example, marriage to them is not an opportunity to explore Christian intimacy but a situation that traps them and makes them vulnerable to someone they don't trust. These people usually view themselves in a highly negative light. They sort of harbor the attitude of old scrooge about Christmas, "bah - humbug." Life is humbug. Marriage is humbug. Church is humbug. Work is humbug. The kids are humbug. And on it goes. You have cynicism on steroids.

Once this view is espoused it is very difficult to recover. You have to throw the cynical attitude about life away and try to see things differently. Contrary to your opinion, life can be incredibly fulfilling and enjoyable. I have always and will always believe that life is what you make of it. If you want life to be bad, it will seem that way to you. If you want life to be good and rewarding, it will be that way to you. Life is not some force that you are just caught up in and have no control over. Life is a gift from God for you to do with it as you see fit in the eyes of God. Your life is not fixed to the extent that you cannot make changes. Do not look at life that way. We live in a world where bad things happen but that does not make the entire universe evil. There is good in this world. There is also good in life. It is all about you and whether or not you want to see it. If you focus on the bad, it is all you will see, but if you look up from where you are, there is plenty of good to behold. Good things like a newborn baby, a successful marriage that was strengthened by adversity, people feeding the poor, or visiting the elderly, seeing a child being baptized into Christ, seeing your dreams come true career wise, a sunrise or sunset, a view of the mountains or oceans, a glimpse of the sky by day and stars by night, and becoming a better person in spite of your past pain. You can see this differently if you want. There is good in life, even on the other side of pain.

Response to Community: God Can Use Your Pain to Heal Someone Else

> And the God of all comfort; who comforteth us in all our affliction so that we may be able to comfort those who are in any affliction which he comfort with which we ourselves are comforted by God... But if we are afflicted, it is for you comfort and salvation; of if we are comforted, it is for your comfort, which is effective in the

> patient enduring of the same sufferings
> which we also suffer" (2 Corinthians
> 1:3-4, 6).

This is one of my favorite passages in the New Testament. It encourages us that even though we have experienced pain, God can help us to overcome it and thus enable us to help others who have been through some of the things we have been through. In other words, God can use your pain to heal someone else. We do have to work with God and first make sure that we are over the pain ourselves. But what a tremendous opportunity we have to help others. Nobody knows what it is like to hurt a certain way like the one who has also walked the walk. Who better knows how to help a depressed person like someone who has overcome depression in their past. Who knows better how to help someone with a troubled marriage like someone whose marriage in the past had some challenges? Who knows what it is like to struggle with alcoholism like a recovering alcoholic, etc.?

If you have been there and recovered, who understands the road to recovery better than you? This is more incentive to get over your pain. Others are hurting who need help and who better to help than you. Let God help you so your affliction can lead to someone else's comfort and salvation from a life of misery and despair. Here are a few ways God can comfort and help you: become one of His children by faith in Jesus Christ, ask God to forgive you of your sins, forgive the ones who hurt you, trust God's will and plan for your life, commit your life to doing good, love your family, love your enemies, let your past be your past, and be concerned about the community you are in. This is all for yours and others best interest. If you let God help you, God will use you to help others. So for all who have been where you are or where you used to be, you can help them find the good life again.

Response to God: It Is Not the End of the World

When we are hurting there is a tendency to act like it is the end of the world. We are so overwhelmed with the pain of the present that we feel incapable of going on any further in life. To the hurting, life is over. To them, "it is the end of the world or life." The one who really suffers from this attitude is God and our relationship with Him. Our logic is, since God allowed me to get hurt, He must not be in control or love me so I am going to stop praying, worshipping him in church, believing in his promises, loving him and others especially my enemies, giving to others and the church, and serving the community. Spirituality as we know it ceases at this point. Whatever has any godly meaning to it gets punished. If someone is hurting enough they will stop coming to church. They will practically shut down spiritually. They think everything is God's fault.

Well here is the truth. God is not to blame for your pain. God gives his creation free-will to make decisions that he will one day judge. God does not put strings on His creation and make them do things. He gives humanity the freedom to act and accept responsibility for the life He has given them. Since God does not make people do things, what they do, be it good or evil, is their choice. It just so happens that bad decisions do cause bad things to people. This is a part of God allowing humans the freedom to live as they fit. But that does not mean God hurt you. God is not to be blamed for the choices people make. If a person does evil, it is their choice. They are to blame for the repercussions, not God. For now, God has decided to allow His creation to make choices and freely interact with one another in good ways and bad ways. However, He is not to blame for people's actions. Blame them and then forgive them but do not pull away from the only real help you have in life. God is your help.

I previously asked what are you going to take from this because I want you to know you have a choice as to how you are going to respond to pain. The manner in which you live, how you interact with others, how you view life, and how you respond to community and God can be done so in a positive light or a negative one. It is your choice. You can take lessons from what you have been through and become a better person or you can be mad at the world and God by being bitter. It is not an easy choice to make. But that choice is yours. I encourage you to take what good you can from what you have been through and let it make you a better person. Let it make you a better father or husband, a better mother or wife, a better Christian, a better employee, a better minister, a better leader in the church, and a better worshipper of God. Remember that becoming a better person is all that is within your power to do. You can overcome whatever tragedy you have faced. Just keep these things in mind.

CHAPTER SEVEN

A WORD TO THE CHURCH

I believe the reason a lot of people do not read the Bible or attend church is because we have made the people of the Bible out to be perfect heroes. Some present them as persons who have never made mistakes, prayed all the time and still had time to keep perfect families. Well that is just not the case. They were ordinary people like you and I, who rose above the circumstances of life and did something unique for God. Great things were done in their lives because they believed in God.

Please know that the people of the Bible were like you and I. The Bible is a book about real life and how to get the most out of the life God has given you. So it is inevitable that even our heroes of faith fought some of the same fights that we face in life. They faced pain, too. I believe it is advantageous for us to study their lives to see how they handled pain. Maybe we will find some tips that will help us in our struggle with pain. Or maybe it will just comfort us to know that they went through some of the things we are going through. And if they survived, we can too.

Let us take a closer look at people's pain in the Bible. Adam and Eve faced a tremendous tragedy. One of their sons murdered his brother, their son. After the murder, he left town for good. So Adam and Eve lost one son in a brutal murder, and the other became a vagabond. I am sure Adam and Eve can tell you about pain. However they did recover by giving birth to another son Seth. They lived through a terrible tragedy, but survived. Hagar knows all too well about the sting of betrayal. Her master's wife Sarah, who was like a friend, suggested that she serve as a surrogate mother for her. Well she consented and gave birth to Ishmael. He was Abraham's first son. All of a sudden, her friend had her own baby and did not want to share the house, nor the attention with Hagar anymore. Even though it was her suggestion, she ordered Hagar and her son out of the house. "Get out" were the sentiments expressed. That had to hurt. Thankfully, God blessed her son and comforted Hagar. They too, lived after pain. Jacob was a pretty good "trickster" who worked for his uncle for seven years so he could receive the love of his life Rachel. However, after those seven years his uncle gave him a woman he did not love. Jacob then had to work another seven years to get the love of his life. Now that is a total of "14" years of suffering and disappointment. That is a long time. But finally he did get the love of his life. Even Jacob found love and joy after years of pain. Joseph can testify to you what it is like to get a little closer to pain. His brothers rejected him because his dad favored him and he was a visionary. This man had big plans for the future. That attitude made his brothers sick. They hated their own brother. So they got rid of him and told their father that he was dead. In all actuality, Joseph was sold into slavery. He spent years in slavery and prison even though he did nothing wrong. Well, the story ends better than it began. Joseph became the overseer of Egypt. He even helped the brothers who tried to destroy his dreams. Joseph made it to the top because he did not let pain get the best of him.

Moses can tell you about pain. He endured many difficulties to help the Hebrews out of Egypt. All they did on that journey back to the Promised Land was complain. One day Moses got mad and lashed out at the people. And for that very reason, God did not allow him to enter the Promised Land. Talk about despair and failure. Imagine what was going on in Moses's mind. "After all I did, this is the thanks I get." Well Moses knows what it is like to fall short of your goal and even be punished for mistakes, but God took care of Moses. What a challenging situation to endure.

David more than anyone in the Bible knows about pain. Look at this summary of some key events of his life. His dad did not recognize him as a son with any potential. His brothers mistreated him. One of his wives thought he was stupid for dancing before the people after the Ark of the Covenant was brought back to Jerusalem. He committed adultery with Bathsheba, had her husband killed and the child born of this union died. His son Absalom betrayed him and was eventually killed and another son for raping his sister. Even God got mad at him but in the end David and Bathsheba's next son Solomon became King of Israel. He was the wealthiest and one of the greatest kings in Israel. Now that is overcoming pain.

Whether it is depression or low self-esteem, the entire scope of human experience from the joys of life to the valley of despair is all in the Bible. Any person on the planet can relate to the Bible because it captures the entire scope of human experience. It serves as a tremendous source of inspiration for anyone because God can help them no matter what predicament in life they face.

If you learn one thing from this it should be that if you keep trying to improve and don't quit, you can experience the good life again. I thank God for these real stories of both sides of life, the good and the bad. I am grateful for believable heroes. Finally, I am encouraged to see that many of them recovered from tragedy and led productive lives. It should let you know that there is life on the other side of pain. So I encourage you to spend time reading and studying these characters and their stories of pain, challenge, ambiguity and triumph. In these stories you will see yourself. Their situations might look and sound like yours. That is a good thing because in the same way they found hope and experienced God, you too, can experience hope and believe anew in the God of second and third and fourth chances.

Stained Glass Windows?

Have you ever wondered why the church used stained glass windows? I mean they seem pointless. No one could see through them into the church and on one could see out of them from within the church. To me it would seem better if the world could see in the church and the church could see outside the church. Therefore the world is reminded of the standard that the church holds in the community, and the church is reminded of the task at hand in reaching the lost with the good news of the gospel of Jesus Christ. But for years, it seemed as if the church did not want the world to really take a good look at them and the church surely did not care about the plight many in the world suffered due to sin. The stained glass window segregated the church from the world.

Today, thank God, stained glass windows are out of style. However, there is a lesson we can learn from the illustration above. During the times stained glass windows were prominent, the church fostered the attitude that they were somewhat better than those on the other side of the stained glass windows. Now everyone knows that Christianity is not about one group of people being better than another group of people but about a perfect lord and savior Jesus Christ. Christianity is about Jesus Christ. But for many years the church possessed sort of an aura of goodness, a gleam of perfection. They had model marriages with compliant children. The local preacher was respected by all in town. Local Christians worked the hardest on their jobs. And the good list goes on and on. I am not saying that ethical living is wrong, because it is not. But what I am saying is that during this time, people's focus was more on people than Jesus. Now the reason I have a problem with this is because people are not perfect in the sense that Jesus is perfect. So what almost destroyed the local Christian witness were persons who allowed society to look at them instead of Jesus, not sins and mistakes made by Christians.

What is important to remember is that even though stained, the window is made of glass and not steel. Ask any kid in the neighborhood who hits a pretty good fastball; windows can be shattered. During the past two decades, the windows across this country have been cracking and breaking. Some of the perfect marriages were a sham. The men were abusive and the wives suffered in silence. Many of the compliant children were so because they suffered abuse for misbehavior. Even the local minister had some problems that once the stained glass was shattered the world saw for the first time. A lot of things the world would never have known were exposed once the stained glass window was shattered. Now the world can see in the church and a lot of what they see disappoints and scares them. But I believe they see what God wants them to see. The church is not a gathering for the elite members of society, or perfectionist who are a few earthly moments from being transfigured. The church is like a hospital where people come sick and get better. The church is not the destination, but the place to come to prepare for it.

The scandals and problems that have surfaced over the past few decades have knocked the church off if its high horse. The world can now see the real church, because the stained glass windows have been shattered. So what is the problem? The problem is the church looking out the shattered stained glass window into the world that sees them for who they really are and that is people who are still in progress. Too many churches are insecure and do not know how to respond now that the cover has been pulled. But I thank God that the cover is blown, because the world has enough phony Christians to last for another millennium. God cannot really be glorified because we are too busy pretending to be angels. Everything will not be perfect until we get to heaven. So we can stop acting like it is so.

The church can really help the world deal with problems when we accept the fact that we wrestle with the same issues, the only difference is that we have Jesus to help us. So many Christians love the comfort the stained glass window gives. They love to pretend that Christians do not have marital problems. They love to pretend that Christian children do not have babies out of wedlock. The love to pretend that preachers are half God and half men like Jesus was, but it is not so. Now I am not condoning immoral behavior, but these things have always been going on. If you do not believe me, read your Bible. They did the same things then, which today we are pretending do not go on in the church.

The apostle Paul told the church at Corinth that they are living epistles known and read by all (2 Corinthians 3:1-2). We are also living epistles known and read by those looking through broken stained glass. Instead of being afraid, we should shine as that city that sits on a hill. We should point people to Jesus who never sinned, nor was guile ever found in his mouth (1 Peter 2:21-22). We should remind the world to come to Jesus with all their hang-ups and problems and trust him to help. After all, that is exactly what Jesus did for us. Instead of hiding behind a false sense of holiness, why not be free to be the person that God is making you to be. By doing this we shift our focus from people to the God who perfects imperfect people one day at a time. Remember, Paul said salvation was possible by the grace of God and not by works, lest any person should boast (Ephesians 2:8). God saves by grace and works in our lives with the same grace that saves us. That is why moral growth and improvement are the result of the grace of God who has enabled us to live a life that is pleasing in his sight and not ourselves. God made it possible because of grace. So the church should be the most open and candid institution in the world because they have all experienced grace and are called to share it with the world. After all, everyone's life is open before God. So what do we have to hide? I believe the greatest encouragement we can give to the world is honesty. Once we understand that God has given the church to help us we can stop acting like we don't need him. Remember that God resists the proud, but gives grace to the humble. So let us look out through those shattered stained glass windows and invite the world to come to the One that helped us out of the same dilemmas in which many face today.

Are We Ready?

As the church of Jesus Christ, we should be able to help virtually anyone with any problem or dilemma. My concern is that we are not. Yes, I believe we are ready for people from other churches to come in with their doctrinal hang-ups but I do not believe we are ready for the hurting masses to come to church. I am talking about the ones we read about doing terrible things on social media, the one on the news guilty of embarrassing activities, the very ones everybody has given up on. When these persons come to church, we have to be ready because they will not be able to hide behind stained glass windows. They have real problems that demand real solutions from real people. I believe this is a job for the church of Jesus Christ.

Remember, let us dispel the notion that everybody in the church is perfect. That is not true. What is true is that people are getting better in the church. Even the people in the Bible dealt with all kinds of issues that would make modern-day Christians blush. Cain murdered his brother.

Noah got drunk and passed out. Lot had sexual relations with both of his daughters. Moses murdered a man. Hosea, the prophet's wife, was a prostitute. David, a man after God's own heart, committed adultery with Bathsheba and had her husband Uriah killed. I am sure the tabloids would have loved to cover some of the events that transpired in biblical times. However troubling these stories seem, God was intricately involved in helping these people deal with life. So if God did this in Old Testament times, we should be doing this today as the church of Jesus Christ. We need to be ready when some of the so-called worst people in society come to church seeking help. The last thing they need is a group of persons who cannot overlook their mistakes and reach out to minister God's love and forgiveness to them.

The church gets so hypocritical at times by acting like the behavior seen in society is something new and shocking. The Bible is full of events that are similar to events that happen today. The Apostle Paul said these things should not even be named among the church. However almost every address to churches in the Bible dealt with issues that are seen in society. Radical behavior is nothing new to society; it's just shocking to witness it on such a large scale. It is not even new to the church. This kind of stuff has been going on for centuries. Ok. Now let's deal with it.

> Come unto me all ye that labor and are heavy laden and I will give you rest (Matthew 11:28).

> Whosoever will, let him take the water of life freely (Revelation 22:17).

89

> Whosoever shall call upon the name of the
> Lord shall be saved (Romans 10:13).

The gospel of Jesus Christ is an invitation. God invites the world to him through his Son Jesus the Christ. This invitation stands at the center of the work that the church carries out in the world. Daily we invite the world to come to Jesus and experience eternal life, joy, peace, forgiveness, understanding and love. Sadly some people in the church want to place limits on who they minister to or allow to come to Jesus. However, God will receive anyone who wants to come to Christ. It doesn't matter what they have done, who they have hurt, or how much society dislikes them. God will receive them if they want help in the person of Jesus Christ. The Bible is clear in telling us that all humanity is the recipient of God's unconditional love (see John 3:16). Therefore, no matter who the person is, God loves them and desires to help them.

The only problem is that the hurting world can only experience the love of God through the people that make up the church. When people in the church decide they want to help some and exclude others depending on what they have done, the world has some major problems. In other words, the church wants to judge. This is wrong. It is not our place to choose who receives God's help. God made that choice for us when he sent Jesus to die for our sins. All we are to do is love the unlovable like God did for us.

Marriages, family relationships, careers and other person's lives at times are in pieces. It is the church's responsibility to help these persons put the pieces of their lives back together again. It is not the church's responsibility to ignore these people but to get down in the mud and help these people put their lives together regardless of the mess they are in. It is not our right to decide who gets help.

> Jesus Christ...hath given us the ministry of reconciliation (2 Corinthians 5:18).

The ministry that we have received from the Lord Jesus Christ is reconciliation. We are supposed to help those who are away from God, find reconciliation with God. Let me repeat myself, God says to his church, "Help the lost find reconciliation through Jesus Christ." The remedy for the ills of hurting humanity is to be reconciled to God. Once reconciled to God, spiritual wholeness will follow. Isn't it time for the church to be doing the business God has called us to do? Let us help the hurting people of the world, whom God loves very deeply, put the pieces of their broken lives back together again.

CHAPTER EIGHT

THE MYTH OF HAVING IT ALL TOGETHER

Have you ever wondered why so many Christians are not as effective for God as they should be? I have and the Lord has helped me to partially understand why this is happening. As long as people walk and live in fear, shame, condemnation, and with overwhelming feelings of inadequacy they will continue to be ineffective vessels in the world for God. This is why it is so important to experience healing. Personal pain tries to keep one so consumed with self-preservation and survival that they ignore the needs of a dying world. This is both a personal faith issue and also one for the church in general. The church has to be careful that our ministerial focus is not solely self-oriented. When the Christian life becomes about me and my issues all the time, how can a dying world be helped. That is why God is calling the church out from this defensive posture to a more offensive mindset as we prepare ourselves to go out into the world with the message of Jesus Christ and the power of the Spirit.

However, not only does the a defensive posture keep us from moving out into the world that Christ sent us into, the myth of a perfect Christian life keeps many believers in a neutral or inactive position in life. You see, the myth of a Christian life that is "all together" keeps all the people who do not have this on the sidelines instead of actively involved in ministry work. I cannot count the times I have heard someone say, when I get it all together then I will get back in church, or when I get it together I will go into the ministry or get more involved. Some of the most anointed people in the body of Christ are on the sidelines or in a waiting room expecting a day to come when everything in their life comes together. Ironically, the devil just keeps bombarding them or plaguing them with life issues that prevent them from reaching this point in life. So what do you do? If you are ever going to be effective in the kingdom of God, you have to learn how to keep moving in God even when everything is not well in life.

Think about this. Isn't it interesting how so many areas of your life can be prosperous according to the principles of God in the word, and yet, there can be one or two areas of your life that are constant sources of pain and adversity. You can look at your marriage and family life and say, this is good. You can look at the career or job that you have and say, this is good. But there is always that area that makes you say, "I need God's help with this." Sometimes even when that problem area is remedied another area of your life falls on hard times. Or things may be well for you but someone you love is going through a difficult time. So there really is never a time when perfection on this side of heaven is achieved. So we have to learn to balance the goodness and blessings of

God with the struggles of life and frailties of being human. I waited for years because I thought God could bring this kind of perfection into my life before I launched out in faith but I only missed wonderful opportunities to be used by God in spite of the difficulties I faced in life. Maybe you know someone like this?

I believe that the wisdom found in Paul's second epistle to the Corinthians can be helpful. This problem has always been in the church. How do we balance a life of goodness and a life of adversity? Paul wanted to help the Corinthians understand that even with the power of God and the gifts of the Spirit difficulty would always be present. The Corinthian church was a gifted church and an immature church. They were so impressed by the charismatic demonstrations of the Spirit that they were misled into believing that their life can be free of adversity. False apostles came in and convinced these immature believers that this was the case and even turned them against Paul. They accused Paul of being a weak and feeble apostle because he did not wield the power of God to his benefit. Therefore his teaching should be discarded and abandoned. Sadly some in the Corinthians church foolishly believed this. He had to write 2 Corinthians to correct the idea that some people wield the power of God.

Today, that kind of theology is still present in the church. Many churches and ministries advocate the same message. Real anointed and faith filled Christians do not have to struggle in life. The power of God is at their disposal to enable them to live above the struggles and trials of life. I have heard forms of that message in churches all over this country. The worst aspect of it is they encourage you to remove yourself from churches and ministries that preach a weak and feeble gospel. They say, get out of those churches that preach doubt and unbelief. Get out of churches that make excuses for a mediocre Christian life. In other words, if you are not walking on water something is wrong with your faith. And it is that kind of preaching that has so many believers on the sidelines because they are not walking on water. So in a manner similar to the Corinthian situation, churches and ministries that proclaim that God's power works in frail vessels find ourselves having to defend our stance. Paul did it in 2 Corinthians and we have to do it today. Super apostles and prophets have deceived many into believing that the power of God is at our disposal and is basically a ticket to the easy life. What did Paul say?

Paul wrote portions of 2 Corinthians to help them understand that God's power works in frail earthly vessels. Effectiveness in the kingdom is a balance or combination of good in life and the difficult. Paul's instructions to the Corinthians best sums up my thoughts.

> But we have this treasure in earthen vessels, that the excellency of the power may be of God, and not of us. We are troubled on every side, yet not distressed; we are perplexed, but not in despair; Persecuted, but not forsaken; cast down, but not destroyed; Always bearing about in the body the dying of the Lord Jesus, that the life also of Jesus might be made manifest in our body. For we which live are always delivered unto death for Jesus' sake, that the

life also of Jesus might be made manifest in
our mortal flesh. So then death worketh in
us, but life in you (2 Corinthians 4:7-12).

Paul argued that God's power in weak earthly vessels
sustains us through all the difficulties of life. The situation
of adversity and struggle is a continual characteristic of
the Spirit-filled life. We suffer adversity but we are never
completely defeated, overwhelmed, or destroyed. Paul stated
that we are always experiencing this "death-like" experience.
The good news lies in the fact that we do not wield the
power of God to escape adversity. The good news is that
God's power preserves us.

In fact, later in this letter Paul argued that the strongest
proof or clearest indicator that God's power was present was
the ability to be sustained through adversity. Not only in
the above passage but also in chapter 12 Paul boasts in the
diverse ways that he suffered, particularly, the thorn in the
flesh that he struggled with. God's power to sustain him in
weakness was worthy of boasting because God's strength
and power was most evident. In the above passage, our
dying and suffering as earthly vessels are clearly to delineate
that what sustains us is God's power. This wonderful ability
gives Christians the opportunity to testify to others who
suffer that God is faithful in spite of adverse situations.

In chapter 1, Paul told the Corinthians how he suffered
almost to the point of death. Look at his description of this
experience.

We were pressed out of measure, above
strength, insomuch that we despaired even

of life; but we had the sentence of death in ourselves, that we should not trust in ourselves but in God that raises the dead: who delivered us from so great a death (1:8-10).

Paul knew what it was like to be at the end of his rope. But his confidence was in God who keeps us from death and is even able to raise us from death. I thank God for believable heroes of the faith. I am so tired of phony Christians with unrealistic testimonies. Give me a hero with strength to overcome adversity, not someone who claims they don't experience adversity because they are so close to God and filled with divine power. When Paul gives us a glimpse of a real Christian life, he lets us know that life can get rough. It is alright. Paul did not feel the need to explain why it is wrong to go through adversity. It is a given fact of life. Job 14:1 says, man that is born of woman is of few days and full of trouble. Psalm 34:19 says, many are the afflictions of the righteous but the Lord delivers him from them all. Even Paul's meditation on ministry in chapter 4 began with the affirmation that adversity should not keep people from faithful ministry. He said, "Therefore seeing we have this ministry, as we have received mercy we faint not" (4:1). Paul knew that God would faithfully keep him in adversity so he persevered. Paul did not wait on the sidelines until everything was together. He learned how to press on in the strength of God. Listen to what Paul endured as a faithful apostle of Christ. Look at how God kept him through situations that would normally overwhelm a person.

I am more; in labors more abundant, in stripes above measure, in prisons more frequent, in deaths often. Of the Jews five times received I forty stripes save one. Thrice was I beaten with rods, once was I stoned, thrice I suffered shipwreck, a night and a day I have been in the deep; in journeyings often, in perils by mine own countrymen, in perils by the heathen, in perils in the city, in perils in the wilderness, in perils in the sea, in perils among false brethren, in weariness and painfulness, in watchings often, in hunger and thirst, in fastings often, in cold and nakedness and through a window in a basket was I let down by the wall, and escaped his hands (11:23-33).

Again it is vitally important to denote that Paul boasted in suffering because God's power was what sustained him. I do not know a lot of Christians who testify about their struggles because they live in a Christian culture that discourages realistic testimony.

Today Paul could not give such a testimony because he would be told that he does not have enough faith. He would be questioned if he was truly an apostle with Holy Ghost power why does he suffers so much. Paul's thorn in flesh would be his answer. He learned by inquiring of God for the removal of a problem that persisted in his life. God's response was not to remove the problem but to give him the grace to be sustained through it. In weakness Paul realized the strength of God, not in ease and comfort. Listen!

> My grace is sufficient for thee: for my strength is made perfect in weakness. Most Gladly therefore will I rather glory in my infirmities, that the power of Christ may Rest upon me. Therefore I take pleasure in infirmities, in reproaches, in Necessities, in persecutions, in distresses for Christ's sake: for when I am weak Then I am strong (12:9-10).

Maybe Paul's humble discovery is the appropriate first step for us to take in dealing with a life of ups and downs. Maybe the pressure of getting it all together can be released if we look to God for strength in the midst of weakness, not in its absence. Paul did not have it all together in the way that many churches and ministries insist for us. Paul could boast, or rather live with his weaknesses and shortcomings because God's strength could overcome human weakness.

I remember the messages preached during my time in Spirit-filled churches in the early nineties. They emphasized God's power in weakness and in spite of difficulties. In other words, the distinguishing characteristic of the Spirit-filled life was perseverance and victory through adversity. God was understood to keep his people and cause us to triumph. I believe that God wants the Spirit-filled church to recover this message from the CEO's that fill pulpits today. And this message has three components to it. First, the devil wants the few areas of your life that are not as well as you would like to take over your life- to be your entire focus. When we are struggling with something the devil wants it to be our sole focus. So many believers are so focused on the few areas of struggle that they neglect or ignore all the areas that God has blessed them. This is a problem because if we are solely focused on the problem areas and not the areas of blessing, our attitude will reflect it. Instead of a positive attitude, they are focused on the struggles and are overly negative. Have you ever met a believer like this? They do not acknowledge the goodness of God and his blessings. They are focused on what God has yet to do for them. Such a posture does not allow a believer to enjoy God's goodness. These people are robbed of joy and peace because their focus is distorted. Celebrating God's goodness in your life empowers you to engage the struggles of life with the right spirit and a fresh zeal. But as long as the devil has you overly focused on your struggles, your mindset will be one that leads to fear, condemnation, shame, and inadequacy. Why? Because your focus is constantly on the areas of your life that have not quite measured up to God's best. There is always something in life worth celebrating. And life is more than one struggle after another. That is why believers have to be balanced. Find something in life to celebrate. You may find that those areas worth celebrating can give you the necessary insight to overcome problem areas of life.

Second, sometimes the areas where we struggle are places where Jesus is yet declared Lord, places that are not fully yielded and obedient to God. Our struggle can be the result of some weakness that we have with sin. The areas of our lives that are not fully yielded to the Lord can cause us to struggle. A favorite sin is a constant temptation because it is hard to give up a sin that we enjoy. We could also have a thorn in the flesh. Some sins or situations are not always directly chosen by someone. Other factors are at work to predispose them to problematic situations or lifestyles like generational curses, economic situations like classism, the Christian's struggle with the flesh, or a personal cross that you have to bear. God works through this complex maze of circumstances to bring his will to fruition in your life. However the constant presence of struggle may point to a problem we have instead of a work that God is doing.

Third, at times God allows and uses these areas; both the good and bad to cultivate various aspects of our lives. When we feel we are facing situations that can have no apparent value or meaning, we must remember that God can take those situations and use them to bless us. For example, in Genesis 50, Joseph came to realize later in his life that a bad situation from an earlier time in life can be beneficial in God's larger plan. However, he did not understand nor appreciate that lesson until it was over. In 2 Corinthians 12, adversity balanced with prosperity helps believers develop spiritual depth. Adversity teaches us more about ourselves than a perpetual state of prosperity. Why? Because strengths should be further cultivated and are further cultivated in the fields of pain and sorrow. That is why it is so futile to believe the myth that true Christians are those who have it all together. That is not the case. God does some of his best work when we are in weakness and do not trust in ourselves. The fields of adversity teach us that we cannot make it without God. They remind us that we must trust in God because the world is uncertain and precarious at best. Situations can change without notice but when God is our source and the rock of our salvation, we can overcome any obstacle that life brings. So child of God, stop wasting your time wishing that everything was perfect in your life. Move forward in God and in faith knowing that God can work with you and is working in you in spite of all the adversity in your life. Stop feeling inadequate. Stop walking in condemnation. Stop feeling sorry for yourself. Start looking to God for what you need and who you are because in him you are complete.

CHAPTER NINE

THE COURAGE TO CHANGE

The church is so quick to point out the increase in immorality that is impacting our communities, churches and families but they often fail to help us understand why people are increasingly leading lives with little to no regard for themselves and others. I do share their concern that we are on the verge of a moral crisis or possibly years into such a crisis. But I do not believe that the only reason people are leading recklessly immoral lives is because they love to sin and live the wild life. Sometimes the church tends to demonize and or romanticize the life of sin. They act like people caught up into self-defeating and destructive lifestyles cannot see what it does to them. Worse yet, they do not believe that people actually want out of these lifestyles. They miss the fact that people somehow feel trapped and do not believe they have a viable alternative and so continue doing what they have always done. When people feel they are trapped and do not see alternate ways to live, they will continue in behaviors, even if it is killing them. Whether it's repeat offenders, young people engaging in risqué behaviors, or the middle class families with excessive credit card debt, people need a viable alternative or they will not change or worse yet grow beyond these things.

What the church has to do is to engage the deeper crisis of meaning that fuels the plunge into moral chaos. And at the root of the moral crisis of our day is a crisis of courage. Society and sadly the church have robbed people of the courage to live moral lives because we have become excessively judgmental and do not provide spaces for imperfect people to grow morally and spiritually. I believe that people want to change but may not always believe they can change. Or maybe they are growing spiritually and in their understanding of how to live a faithful life before God. It is the church's job to nurture the belief that with God change is always possible and that change leads to growth. Let me ask a few questions. If you have sinned in the past does it mean that you are cursed or perpetually stuck in this condition? Does sin forever define you? If you move on and believe in truth and righteousness, does it mean you are a hypocrite? The answers are simple. No- a person is not cursed or perpetually stuck in a condition of sin. No- sin does not forever define a person. No- a person is not a hypocrite because they refuse to allow past sins to define them. The answers are simple but sadly, many in the church treat people in ways that suggest the answers to these questions are yes. If the church is going to do this we have to deal with two major problems. The people in our churches and communities who try to define people by their sin pose one problem and the belief people in church are hypocrites because they are imperfect is the second problem. I believe that there is wisdom in the story of the prodigal son and

Jesus' criticism of the hypocrisy of the Pharisees that can shine some much needed light on this.

Those Who Won't Let You Move On

I begin with the story of the prodigal son because it underscores the challenges of change, especially as it relates to those around you who will not let you move on. I believe that it is hard to change. Anyone who tries to tell you that change is easy is not being honest. Change is hard but not impossible. So what we have to do is identify and deal with the things that make change difficult. This will pave the way for us to experience lasting change. One of the things that complicates change is moving on after you have sinned, after you have made a mistake of some kind. When you have messed up the temptation is to wallow in self-pity and contempt. There are some people whose life gets worse after they mess up because they will not move on and start a new chapter in life. Why do people refuse to move on? I believe one reason is that it requires courage to move on with your life. You see courage is an aspect of morality often neglected by the church. To truly be moral one has to grow. And many times growth comes after hard lessons in life.

That is why I admire the courage of the prodigal son. He admitted his wrong. In addition to this, he made the decision not to allow this episode to define him. Because he was did not allow this episode to define him, he was able to begin the next chapter of his life on his own terms. Luke 15 says "and he came to himself." What this signifies is the prodigal son seeing through eyes that were formerly blinded by pride and ambition. Once his eyes were opened he decided to go back to his father's house. There are two important life lessons we can draw from this courageous act. First, sometimes going back is the best way to go forward. The prodigal son decides he is not going to spend his life running away from what he had done. It is only after making peace with his past that they can truly write a new chapter. Second, by going back, he takes responsibility and ownership for the next chapter of his life instead of leaving it to his skeptics. What he did required a tremendous amount of courage because it is hard to admit wrong and face up to the consequences of your actions. That is why I am writing this. I want to emphasize the courage required to repent. I also want to encourage the church to recover its role as agents of genuine change when we provide space for people to repent and celebrate the courage required to do so. Yes, I said celebrate. Luke 15:7, 10 reminds us that there is joy in heaven when one sinner repents and the angels in heaven rejoice when one sinner repents. If heaven takes notice of the act of repentance and celebrates it, then the church should do the same thing on earth. This will change the cultures of our churches and allow change to naturally, or should I say, to spiritually take its course in our lives.

Instead our churches have cultures that discourage change because we do not allow people to move on. Jesus says there is joy in heaven when one sinner repents but the truth is there is not always joy on earth. Jesus says the angels rejoice when one sinner repents but there are some people on earth who get upset when one sinner repents. In this story, we encounter a person who is not happy that the prodigal son "came to himself" and decided to return to his father's house. In fact, this person is so upset that he refuses to join the celebrations going on both in heaven and in the house of this father. He is referred to in Luke 15 as the eldest brother. This brother signifies the people who do not want you to move on and people who are not joyful when you repent. Worse yet, these people feel cheated when God forgives a sinner. Here is what the eldest brother misses. God loves sinners and will leave the ninety-nine for the one lost sheep.

Because Jesus, as the good shepherd who searches for lost sheep, I read Luke 15:17 in a totally different light. When this verse says "and he came to himself" I believe that he did so because God was at work in his heart. I used to believe this verse implied that the prodigal son finally saw the error of his ways and decided to change on his own. But the truth is you don't come to yourself by yourself. You come to yourself because God is at work in you and around you. It is this work that makes repentance possible. Because God convicts and calls us to our better selves, we respond first by repenting, which is acknowledging how we have fallen short of that call and second by living better going forward. God is the one who opens our blind eyes and enables us to see just how much we need to change. Because God was at work, the prodigal son confessed that he sinned against heaven and his father. The eldest brother ignores the work of God in bringing this lost son home. And the reason he ignores this is because his eyes are just as blind as his little brothers were in 15:12. The only difference is that he stayed home. It's hard to change by yourself. You need somebody to recognize and believe in the new you.

The church should take up this work. This story is significant because it underscores the importance of supporting the change in other people. The father and all those in the household who celebrated the son's return did this. They represent the kind of church that can help people to change and to grow. The eldest brother did not do this. And he represents the kind of church that keeps people stuck in the past and leaves them with no alternative but more of the same sin that ruined their lives in the first place.

The Accusation of Being a Hypocrite

The second issue is what to do about the issue of hypocrisy. It is a popular criticism that "everybody in church is a hypocrite." People in church have heard this charge in barbershops, grocery stores, street corners, and family reunions for years. What the criticism is getting at is the gap between what people in church profess and how they live. In other words, people in church say one thing but do another.

But what the criticism fails to understand is the courage required to become a Christian in the first place. In most churches, becoming a Christian is both a private and public act. This action consists of a confession of one's sins and to ask for God's forgiveness to basically save you from your sinful self. Doing this privately in prayer and publicly in confession is a courageous act. The criticism also misses that even converted Christians are imperfect. They are transformed spiritually but are still very much a work in progress. This means that Christians will have obvious shortcomings and sins that they take to church with them. Just because they are imperfect does not mean they are hypocrites. However, this is not to say that people in church cannot be hypocrites because they can and we all know there are some hypocrites in the church.

Here in Matthew 23, we see Jesus come down hard on religious leaders for their hypocrisy. What is so problematic for Jesus is not that these leaders are imperfect but that they pretend to be more than they really are. I like to say it like this. You are not a hypocrite for being imperfect. You are a hypocrite when you claim to be somebody you are not. Jesus begins with the general charge that the Pharisees do not practice what they preach. Verse 3 reveals that hypocrites only talk the talk. Jesus said that the Pharisees say but fail to do. They talk the talk but fail to walk the walk. The real problem with this is that they take the time and expend the mental energy to learn what is right but do so having no intention of doing it. To expand our understanding of hypocrisy further look at verses 4-7. Jesus exposes how hypocrites love to look righteous. Their good works are a show put on to draw attention to themselves and to gain recognition. They are not concerned about doing good for the right reasons. They focus on the benefits such actions have for them. Then Jesus goes on to warn how hypocrites try to influence others. In verses 13-15, Jesus goes on to show how hypocrites go out of their way to convert others but in the end their converts become a child of hell just as the hypocrite is.

In Matthew 23, the Greek word for hypocrite signified a "play actor" or one who plays a part on stage. It also signified outward show or someone who was a pretender. The Jewish usage of this word is revealing. In Jewish literature the hypocrite presents a righteous appearance so that their true face of evil is disguised. This aspect of hypocrisy is what Jesus identifies as so problematic in the last half of Matthew 23. Jesus was so upset because the cloak of righteousness masks an inward evil that is not easily discernable by the masses of people. In verse 23-24, Jesus is upset because the Pharisees hide behind rules and minutia because they do not want to do what is right. The Pharisees give careful attention to tithing but ignore justice and mercy. Jesus challenges a form of piety that is preoccupied with minutia and ignores issues that are more significant- caring for widows and orphans and the poor. The Pharisees ignore these people. In verses 25-28, Jesus takes them to task for their preoccupation with outward cleanliness while being inwardly unclean and dead. He shows how hypocrites prioritize outward righteousness and completely ignore inward righteousness. For them it is about appearance and not substance.

What we see in these scriptures is that the real problem with the hypocrite is not just that they do not practice what they preach but who they really are. A true hypocrite is an evil person disguised as a righteous person. Jesus' criticism teaches us two important lessons. We should be careful about trying to look righteous or to act righteous. Instead we should commit ourselves to being righteous as we faithfully try to obey God's commands. We should also be honest about who we are and where we are in life. Honesty is always the best way to fight hypocrisy. The popular criticism of Christians as duplicitous or two faced persons who do not practice what they preach while accurate of some Christians is too broadly applied and misses important aspects of lifelong changes we undergo. The charge of hypocrisy robs people of the moral courage that is essential in lasting and authentic change.

Humans are not perfect. They are deeply flawed individuals who construct deeply flawed societies. It is because of God's love and power that humans are able to escape the hopeless cycle of defeat and death to sin. And not only are humans imperfect, but Christians are imperfect too. God transforms us and calls us to live a life of unfolding transformation. This takes time. So we patiently live out the life of faith and experience transformation incrementally. In this sense, the church is the place where we are instructed, nurtured, and supported in the life of faith. The church is the place where Christians "together" experience incremental and steady moral improvement. And so the church must guard itself from beliefs and practices that rob people of the courage to undertake seriously the life of transformation that God calls every person to. The gospel is good news about Jesus Christ and his saving power that transforms us. The gospel is good news because it does not let sin have the final word over our lives. God's power triumphs over sin's power and gives us hope and the power to change, to grow, and to be strengthened. May we undertake this work in our churches and in our preaching.

CHAPTER TEN

CAN ANYBODY STOP THE PAIN?

Rarely does a day pass in which we are not reminded that people are hurting. Many times we find ourselves in awe as we watch the nightly news and witness a society violently out of control. At first it was just subtle reminders like nations at war with one another over political agendas, an occasional violent murder that gained national attention, a hijacking of some kind or even a random case of child abuse. For some time mainstream society grew accustomed to these incidents because they were random. Then things changed dramatically. The last two decades of the twentieth century and the first decade of the twenty-first century have witnessed an avalanche of violence, tragedy and pain unsurpassed by any time in history.

Today the twenty-four news cycle and social media tell us that children are killing children. Teenage girls are mothering children. Women are being raped daily. Racism is still a major problem. The divorce rate is too high. Infidelity threatens too many relationships. School teachers are having sex with children. Suicide is still one of the leading causes of death in America. Drug and alcohol abuse continue to devastate people's lives, families and communities. And the list goes on and on. I know many people who wonder as I have on many occasions, "Can anything be done to stop this?" Well I believe this book is a small part of long process that this country needs to turn things around. I do believe that it is within our power to make things better. Many people admit that America needs a change but few are committed to changing things in their lives and the lives of those around them. If change is going to come about it will do so one individual at a time.

I have been given the tremendous opportunity of sharing this message with you. This message can begin a process of change if it begins with you. If this message changes some part of your life and brings healing to your life, you can become a part of the much needed change this country needs. After having read this book, I challenge you to look at yourself with the goal of trying to make some changes. Because if change is going to come about it is going to start with you, not your spouse, preacher, mayor, governor or president. Change should always begin with you. You see, if you change a part of the world has changed.

After reading this book you should realize your life matters. You should realize that your life counts for something. So if you live in a way that is pleasing to God, change will occur and the turn around that this nation so desperately needs can be realized one individual at a time. Everybody has been hurt. I have been hurt. And we have all in some way or another hurt someone else because of our pain. I pray this book will help you come to grips with the pain of your past and also to overcome its effect on your life. God can use your pain to help others who cannot cope. So when you see someone wounded in life you can say "here let me help you. I have been through that myself." Well I am sure you have been challenged by some of the things discussed in this book. If some things hit close to home seriously consider making some changes in your life. Remember it is within your power to become a better person and recover from past pain. The pain can be stopped.

Will Thou Be Made Whole?

This is undoubtedly one of the most interesting healing stories in the Bible. A man comes to Jesus in need of healing and is asked "will thou be made whole? (John 5:6)" You would think every sick person wants to get better. Yet Jesus asks him if he wants to get better. The man, who is described as impotent for thirty-eight years, says he doesn't have anyone to carry him to the pool so he can be healed. Jesus told him to take up his bed and walk. He was miraculously healed. This story teaches us a valuable lesson. It teaches us that wholeness is something within our power to attain and one of the things needed for healing is the desire and willingness to get better. You have to want it. Jesus did not just force healing on this man. And today Jesus helps those who want help. If you are really going to get better you need to ask yourself do you really want to get better? Because if you don't have the desire to get better you will continue to live hurt and feel sorry for yourself. But if you want wholeness you will be committed to the road to recovery no matter how long it may take you to complete it.

Maybe you are wondering what exactly is wholeness. Wholeness is completeness, a person who is sound spiritually, emotionally, and psychologically. Wholeness means there are no big cracks in our personhood. Wholeness is also recovery from past pain. It is a person who has taken advantage of the second chance they got in life. It is also being a good person when you used to be a bad one. Wholeness is where everything works like it's supposed to work. So many times people who have been hurt like to sit around and be sad expecting someone to come along and make their pain go away. But my question to you is "Do you want to get better?" And if you want to get better then you have to get up and help yourself by facing the pain and getting some help. You have to admit that you need help. Did you catch that? You have to admit that you need help. No one can help you if you deny the fact that you need help. If you want to get better then you need to make some things happen for yourself.

A New Vision for the Future

Earlier in the book we discussed how hurting people hurt people. Now let us move to a more promising end. A new vision for the future is a world where whole people help hurting people. It is a world where we are our brother's and sister's keepers. It is a vision of a world where we care about our neighbors. What this world needs are people who have recovered from the pain of life and are willing to help others. We have enough people who want to spread their pain. What we really need are people who want to help hurting people. This is how we can make a big difference in the world we all live in. We get over our pain and spend the rest of our lives helping others get over their pain.

Try It Again

Maybe you just hit rock bottom. Maybe you are at the bottom of the barrel. Maybe you are out of options. Maybe you have nowhere to go but up. This lowly junction in your life may be the most important one for you. What you do now will determine the direction of your life for the better or for the worse. Life at the bottom can be very sobering. You wonder how did you ever get here or how this could have happened to you. Maybe you are asking yourself how did I end up in jail, or pregnant, or homeless, or in divorce court or alone contemplating suicide. There are not a lot of people who would help you but Jesus can help you and wants to help you. In this desperate junction of your life reach out to him. Jesus Christ can come where you are and help you. You do not have to die. You do not have to spend the rest of your life down and out. You can get up.

Look at the prodigal son in Luke 15. He had everything. He was part of a wealthy family and had a father who loved him. But he decided to throw it all away. You know the story. He took his inheritance and left home. After a time of partying and enjoying the wild life he found himself without money. The good times quickly came to an end. This rich kid had to get a job where the pay was very low, so low the he desired the scraps of food that he was feeding the pigs. That is rock bottom. The prodigal son tells you about rock bottom, about being down and out. But the most wonderful thing happened to him. The Bible said that at that low point in his life he came to himself. Afterwards, he went home to his family and loving father. That is what you do. You can come home. Jesus can show you the way. I know what you are thinking. I can even sense the sarcasm and resentment you feel at the thought of giving your life a second chance. Try it again.

> Now when he had left speaking, he said unto Simon, launch out into the deep and let down your nets for a draught (catch). And Simon answering said unto him, master we have toiled all the night and have taken nothing: nevertheless at thy word I will let down the net (Luke 5:4-5).

The disciples can somewhat empathize with you about the difficulty of trying something that has previously failed. I can really sense the frustration of Simon as he explained that they have tried to catch fish all night and haven't caught anything. He told Jesus, "We have toiled all night and have taken nothing." Whatever they were doing was not working and it was very frustrating. It is hard to try again when you have invested so much of yourself in a particular endeavor or relationship. Personal energy is a valuable commodity. And when its use yields nothing, a second or third attempt seems pointless. Why keep trying to make it work when it has failed in the past?

Maybe there is a different way to think about this. Other obstacles that keep us from trying are failed plans and sincere intentions that did not benefit you. Society teaches us "if you fail to plan you plan to fail." So you develop a plan for your life, or career or your marriage and it still failed. This can be devastating. You constantly tell yourself this cannot be because I had a good plan. Things were not supposed to turn out this way. Trying again now seems to be a very daunting task to a person whose plans just failed. An even greater obstacle is when your intentions in life were sincere and yet you still failed. So many times society says "nice guys finish last" and that quote echoes in the back of a mind whose good intentions got them nowhere. It is a bitter pill to swallow when you have done the right thing and ended up with the wrong result. You are not thinking about trying again except maybe being the bad guy or gal again. At least you could get ahead. However, probably the two most daunting obstacles to overcome are trying again when others know you have failed and trying again when it looks hopeless. Personal shame is a powerful obstacle. It is one thing to fail in a personal area of your life but an entirely different thing when others know about it. Shame's powerful motivational influence will attempt to keep you in hiding for the rest of your life. It is hard to face people when you have failed in any area of your life. Whether it's your marriage, your job, your financial stability or your integrity, trying again is difficult. Still I encourage you to try again.

I encourage you to resist the tendency to become self-absorbed in a prison of pity and defeat. This can easily become a lifestyle. Do not allow your entire focus to center around your failures and mistakes. The devil wants you to spend the rest of your life beating yourself up. I can hear him whispering in your ear, "you are a failure" or "you have ruined your life." Do not listen to those voices. Jesus wants you to focus your energies and your faith in his plan for your life that cannot fail. Remember the last thing Simon said, "Nevertheless at thy word I will let down my net." Upon doing this a boatload catch of fish was made. You see wonderful things can happen when people obey the word of God.

Just like those frustrated disciples on the sea catching nothing, our lives do not work properly or give fulfillment until we listen to Jesus. We can try real hard, have good intentions and plans but without the Lord's blessing, it will not work. Our world is filled with frustrated people whose lives do not work the way they would like them to. Maybe you realize that you are in that situation. What do you do? Follow the example of the prodigal son and "come to yourself." Wake up. Get the picture! Figure it out! You need to go home and Jesus Christ is the way home.

Who Can Stop the Pain?

> "Come unto me all ye that labor and are heavy laden and I will give you rest (Matthew 11:28)."

> "I come that they might have life and have it more abundantly (John 10:10)."

If you are sincerely tired of struggling with some of the issues discussed in this book maybe you need to see for yourself what Jesus has to offer. Do not misunderstand me. I am not offering you religion but a living relationship with a living God and a living savior who promises to be with you until the end of the age. I am offering you a personal relationship with Jesus Christ. The death of Jesus Christ paid the penalty for your sin and your pain. By trusting in Jesus Christ you can be saved from your sins and receive a real second chance in life. He is not six-steps to emotional wholeness but he is the only one who can stop your pain and heal your life. I do not want you to misunderstand what I have been trying to do in this book. All the advice in the world will not bring healing to your life if you do not know Jesus Christ. He is the source of healing and peace for all in the throes of pain. Jesus is alive today and that reality will enable you to experience the good life one day at a time. Before you know it Jesus will have turned your pain into victory and bitterness into medicine for others who have been hurt.

APPENDIX:
QUESTIONS AND ANSWERS

Question 1: What is your advice to hurting people?

My advice is "avoid quick fixes from anyone promising overnight or instant healing from traumatic experiences." Healing takes time. Do not risk your future happiness and mental health on quick fixes. Real pain isn't an instantaneous thing. It is the product of months and sometimes years of hurt in the heart of an individual. Therefore real healing will not be instantaneous. Take your time and fully recover. God is more concerned about the process of healing rather than someone's formula for a painless life. Again, I stress that you take your time.

Question 2: What advice do you have for someone who wants to give up or even commit suicide?

Life can be so difficult at times that it tempts a person to give up. Life can be hard and there are some places in life that are so hard that one can be tempted to even end their own life. I admit that life is hard. I do not want to underestimate your pain but giving up is not a real solution. It doesn't solve anything for you and the people you love.

It only makes it worse. So my advice to you is to keep struggling and fighting through this season in your life. Even though you may think the world would be better off without you, such thinking is wrong and will lead you down the wrong path. If you did not have any value, God would not have created you and given you a purpose in life. You do have value. I will tell you this. The world would be better off if you improve rather than give up on life. Suicide is not the solution to your problem. The solution is a commitment to improvement. Life can be better for you. My final word to you would be if you have been having suicidal thoughts or thoughts of harming yourself then please get help. Call a trusted family member, friend or pastor and tell them to take you to see a therapist or mental health professional. They can help you get the next chapter of your life off on the right foot.

Question 3: What advice would you have for someone who is unwilling to forgive someone for a past mistake?

The first thing I would say is that whoever hurt or wronged you was wrong. You have every right to be upset, angry, disappointed and sad. Nobody likes being taken advantage of or lied to or mistreated or abused. Nobody! But I do not want you to spend the rest of your life dwelling on and internalizing these feelings. I will not try to encourage you to let them go. So the question is how? This leads me to my next point. Everyone makes mistakes. Nobody is perfect. I wish everyone would understand this when someone else is on the other end of needing forgiveness. I admit that it is hard to forgive someone who has really hurt you. However, if you realize that you have hurt God more times than you would care to count yet he forgave you when you sought forgiveness. Remember how refreshed you were to be forgiven for your mistakes? Remember what it felt like to get a fresh start with God? There is no feeling like being forgiven. It is truly liberating. If you remember this then why should you not do the same for the person or persons who wronged you? People who make mistakes on the most part will make good on a second chance. You think that you will not ever need to be forgiven for anything but if you did, would you want a second chance? Sure you would. Then do for that person what you would like done if the shoe was on the other foot.

Question 4: What is the most difficult aspect of being the bad person or perpetrator in a painful situation?

I believe it is rejection. No one likes to be rejected. But when a person does wrong or hurts someone, rejection is an inevitable response and reaction by others. Most people do not know how to return good for evil. They usually resort to an "eye for an eye," which is form a retaliation. People tend to reject those who hurt them. They reject them because they have been burned one too many times. They reject people because they lost respect and can no longer trust the one who hurt them. The downside to being rejected is that it results in further alienation. People who hurt others are wrong but they need people in their lives to care for, love them and hold them accountable. That is why rejection is so dangerous for people like this. It threatens to push them deeper into their dysfunction and further away from people who can help them. Listen up. If you have hurt someone, people are going to reject you. However, you should not use their rejection as an excuse for your irresponsible and hurtful actions. And you shouldn't use their rejection as a crutch to lean on for the rest of your life. You can turn this situation around with God. Here's how. First, repent to God for what you have done to him and others. Ask God for forgiveness with a contrite heart. Then open your heart to the love and grace of God, which will help you rebuild your life and confidence. In spite of other people's feelings about you and what you did, be patient, understanding and kind to them anyway. It is a healthy part of you accepting the responsibility for your actions. Then I would challenge you to use your mistakes to motivate you to become a better person. If you have sincerely changed the people who rejected you and refused to believe in you may give you another chance. But even if they will not ever accept you again, you should improve your life because it is the right thing to do. You cannot just wallow around in defeat for the rest of your life. You have to get up and do the best you can with what is left of your life. You may have deserved to be rejected but you do not have to let it define the rest of your life.

Question 5: How do you help a person who doesn't want to admit they need help?

You cannot do anything for someone who does not want help. However, establishing some boundaries with them and being kind and loving to that person will be a good dose of medicine. Accountability, structure and love can be therapeutic for hurting people. Most people have to decide if they want to improve their quality of living. No one else can do it for them. Be kind, and by all means, pray for them. The thing to really pray for is that your kindness will motivate them to want to do better. Also remember that some people improve the way they live when they see genuine change and kindness in someone else. So be sure that you improve and change as you expect the other person to do so.

Question 6: How do Christians get through tough times?

I could go on for days to answer this but I will summarize it this way. We get through tough times because God is with us. Christians rely on the presence of God. If it were not for God being present with his people, there would be more despair and death then this world could ever imagine. We also get through tough times because of God's love. God's love and mercy gets us through situations that would break down the strongest person. Because we know God loves us and is helping us, even though we don't fully understand how, we have faith that things will work out. That is how we get through those times that tempt us to throw in the towel. We do not get through times because we are smart or strong. We are not as wise as we think and we are certainly not as strong as we think we are. Tough times test us like nothing else and during those times, many of us realize that "had it not been for the Lord who was on our side, where would we be?"

Question 7: Does God remove difficulty from the lives of his people?

It is not so much that God removes difficulty from the lives of his people but more that God helps his people to the extent that adverse situations do not seem that bad anymore. In other words, God equips us for trouble instead of moving it out of our lives. Many Christians look back over their lives and wonder how they have survived tragedies and difficulties and yet still have joy and peace of mind. We are able to smile and to face the challenges of today because God helps us to bear up under the worse of circumstances.

Question 8: What advice would you give to someone experiencing a broken relationship?

I would say that you are not alone. There are many people today who know about the pain of a broken relationship. Even the people in the Bible were not immune to problems in relationships. People such as Jacob, Rachel, Leah, Hosea, Gomer and the Samaritan woman of John 4 all experienced the pain of difficult and broken relationships. You are not alone and your pain is similar to these people, though they are thousands of years removed from your particular situation. I would also say that a broken relationships is a different type of pain to experience because it involves another person. And it is not just another person but someone you love, probably very deeply at a point in the relationship. So the pain of love gone wrong and a relationship breaking up is very upsetting. In fact, a broken relationship can turn your life upside down and inside out. The reason it does so is because there is such a myriad of conflicting feelings about the relationship. Part of you still loves the person. Part of you does not. You remember the good times yet cannot forget all the bad times. You are frustrated and disappointed that the relationship did not work. You resent them. You are hurt. You are hesitant and unsure about a lot of things in life. And you are fearful about your future. Broken relationships are difficult with all these emotions involved. You have all these feelings but remember your life is not over and you are alone. God is with you and I am certain you have a few family members and friends you can lean on during this time.

Question 9: What advice would you give to someone experiencing loneliness?

Is there any worse a punishment than loneliness? Being completely isolated and alone is a difficult and painful experience. People need interaction and relationship in order to thrive spiritually and emotionally. After all God said in Genesis that "it is not good for man to be alone." One of the greatest ironies today is that in a world of over six billion people, so many people are lonely. And this loneliness affects our society in many ways. This sense of loneliness feeds intense feelings of emptiness. So many that I have counseled and ministered to in church reveal such a deep sense of emptiness rooted in feelings of loneliness. They feel that their lives have some kind of void that has not been filled. What ends up happening is that some try to fill the void with alcohol or drug abuse, illicit sex, eating, shopping or even by throwing themselves into their career. Eventually these things become habits and addictions that only cause more problems like affairs, divorce, rape, pornography, workaholism, even violence. My advice would be to invest in quality and godly friendships. Isolation is not a good thing, especially for someone hurting. You need to get some good people around you to support you, care for you, get to know you and love you for the unique person that you are.

Printed in the United States
By Bookmasters